THE
GREENWICH VILLAGE
GUIDE

Sixteen Historic Walks · Includes Soho,
Tribeca, and the East Village

Antique Shops, Bookstores, Theatres,
Clubs, Restaurants, Art Galleries, and More

FRED W. McDARRAH AND PATRICK J. McDARRAH

a cappella books

a cappella books
an imprint of
Chicago Review Press, Incorporated

Editorial offices:
P. O. Box 380
Pennington, NJ 08534

Business/sales offices:
814 N. Franklin St.
Chicago, IL 60610

Cover photographs by Fred W. McDarrah
Top: The New Museum
Middle: Washington Square Park
Bottom: The Philip Glass Ensemble

Disclaimer

Although every effort was made to ensure the accuracy of the information appearing in this book, readers are advised that establishments may move or close over the course of time. The authors and publisher cannot be held responsible for the experiences of the reader using this guide. Readers are invited to write the publisher with ideas, comments, and suggestions for future editions.

Library of Congress Cataloging-in-Publication Data

McDarrah, Fred W., 1926–
    The Greenwich Village guide : fifteen historic walks : includes Soho, Tribeca, and the East Village / Fred W. McDarrah and Patrick J. McDarrah.
        p.   cm.
    ISBN 1-55652-151-0 : $11.95
    1. Greenwich Village (New York, N.Y.)—Guidebooks.   2. New York (N.Y.)—Guidebooks.   3. Walking—New York (N.Y.)—Guidebooks.
I. McDarrah, Patrick J.   II. Title.
F128.68.G8M36   1992
917.47'10443—dc20
                                                            92-27916
                                                            CIP

Contents

Introduction

If the great chronicler of *The Decline and Fall of the Roman Empire*, Edmund Gibbon, were to write a guidebook, it would probably turn out a lot like *The Greenwich Village Guide*. Like Gibbon's volume, this book is meticulously researched. It's chockful of names, dates, and addresses, stocked with hard-to-find or never-before-seen photos, and, best of all, it's a pretty good read. I've seen a lot of guidebooks about New York and specifically the downtown neighborhoods of Greenwich Village, the East Village, Soho, and Tribeca. This is the best one.

No, I am not impartial about this. The original edition of this book, which came out in 1963, was dedicated to me, "Timothy Swann, a native Villager." I was one year old. For this edition, my dad and brother wrote most of the text and my mom did some additional writing.

Now, I'm a reporter for the *New York Post* and live with my photographer wife, Caroline Howard, a few minutes from where I was born on Thompson Street. Back then, it was a rough-and-tumble Italian neighborhood; today it's chic Soho. But that makes me even more qualified to pass judgment here. I know better than anyone else that this book, for lack of a better cliché, is a true labor of love. Research on this volume did not begin when the authors signed a contract to write it. Instead, it began decades ago, when my parents arrived here from Brooklyn and the Bronx.

Sure, there's pounds of book research and historical oddities on the pages to come. You'll find out that General Tom Thumb was married at Grace Church on Fourth Avenue and 10th Street. You'll be directed to the building where the great Civil War photographer Matthew Brady took Abraham Lincoln's portrait. If you want to drink where Pete Hamill, Jackson Pollock, Willa Cather, Dylan Thomas, or Max Eastman hoisted a few brews, the names and addresses of the bars are provided.

Bits and pieces of that information can be found in plenty of other books. The reason that this book is special is not only because it incorporates three centuries of facts into one handy volume, but it draws on life experiences. My parents did not take notes every time they had a beer at the old Cedar Street Tavern with artists from the New York School like Franz Kline or Bill de Kooning. My mom never wrote a magazine article about the day Jack Kerouac came over and she typed a poem the two of them worked on. But tidbits like these, and thousands of others, contribute substantially to the overall tone and content that make this a superior book. (Plus, I learned a little more about my own family. For example, until I read the manuscript, I never knew my grandfather, Lou Schoffel, was canned from the Triangle Shirtwaist Company a few days before the fatal fire.)

An opportunity to interact with people like Norman Mailer, Bob Dylan, or Robert De Niro (or less famous but equally fascinating characters) is the reason people still flock to Greenwich Village and the surrounding neighborhoods of Soho, the East Village, and Tribeca. The reason people come here is to be a part of things: things as they were, things as they are, and things as they are yet to be.

Sure, things change. The Village is not what it used to be. There are no more cheap rooming houses on Washington Square South. The Sixth Avenue El has been down for years. Rents for studio apartments are $1000.00 a month. The Waldorf Cafeteria closed decades ago. Maxwell Bodenheim, John Reed, Joe Gould, and Phil Ochs are long dead.

But the Village is also exactly what it has always been. Unknown folksingers try to hit it big on MacDougal Street. Street artists still hang their paintings from clotheslines and hope some big dealer notices them. Balducci's still has the best produce. Students from all over the city still get stoned in Washington Square Park. It is still where e. e. cummings and Henry James wrote some of their best works.

No neighborhood on earth can match the energy, history, and mystique of Greenwich Village. After spending some time here—with, of course, this book as your navigator—you'll know exactly why.

Timothy S. McDarrah

Lower New York (overview)

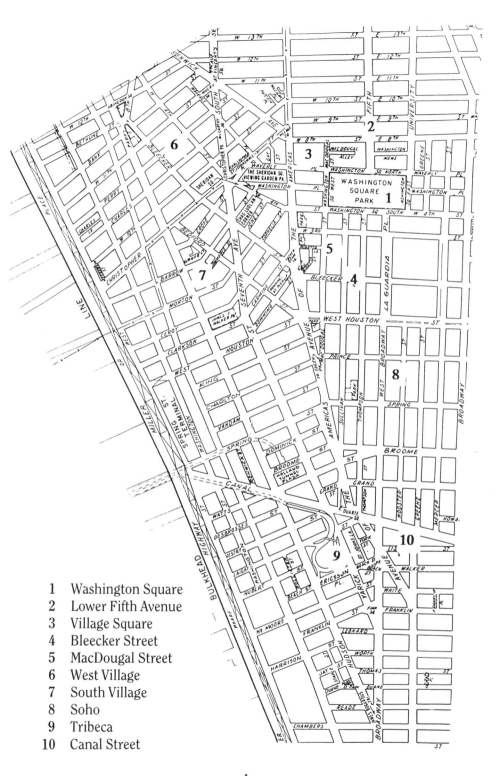

1 Washington Square
2 Lower Fifth Avenue
3 Village Square
4 Bleecker Street
5 MacDougal Street
6 West Village
7 South Village
8 Soho
9 Tribeca
10 Canal Street

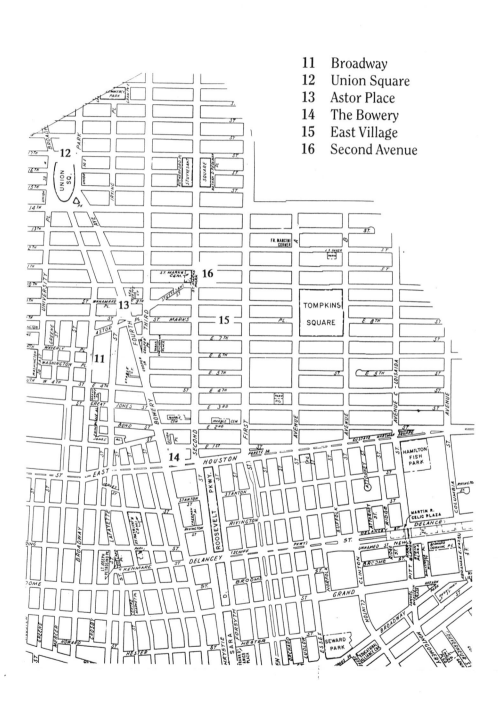

11 Broadway
12 Union Square
13 Astor Place
14 The Bowery
15 East Village
16 Second Avenue

Greenwich Village: Past and Present

Green Village; Under the Dutch; Smallpox Plagues; Village Settlers; Bohemian Tradition; Tea Rooms and Rendezvous; Cradle of Countercul-ture; Free Love — Free Speech; Radical Literary Publications; Tourist Market; Surreal Characters; Economic Bonanza

For 100 years, Greenwich Village has been the liveliest and most colorful community in New York. An exciting complex of interesting people, fascinating places, and dynamic ideas, the Village has the vitality of a metropolis, the intimacy of a neighborhood, and a personality all its own.

The arbitrary boundaries of the Village are from Spring Street to 14th Street and from the Hudson River to Second Avenue; the center of Greenwich Village is Washington Square, an eight-acre park that is four city blocks in size.

On the side streets and twisting alleys of the Village, there is a bewildering variety of espresso cafés, art galleries, off-Broadway theatres, nightclubs, famous bars, and avant-garde bookshops. If you desire to explore historic treasures, you'll find that the Village is interwoven with more buildings, streets, and landmarks with histori-cal significance than any other community of its size in America.

Greenwich Village began with the arrival of the Dutch explorer Henry Hudson in 1609. Before the European's discovery of the island

1

of Manhattan, the area was inhabited by Sapokanikan Indians. Their land amply supported their needs: game was plentiful in the rich forest, and the pure river waters supplied their fish. It was the sheer abundance of the game that attracted Hudson's notice. On his return to Holland, he praised New York's natural resources so loudly that the government chartered the Dutch West India Company in 1621 to send fur traders to the island and gave the Company rights of commerce for what they called "New Netherlands."

The first Dutch governor, Wouter Van Twiller, took office in 1633. He claimed as his personal estate the entire section inhabited by the Sapokanikans, stretching from Minetta Brook to the Hudson River, and called it "Bossen Bouwerie," which he developed into a tobacco farm. Later he also claimed what are now Governor's Island, Ward's Island, Randall's Island, and Staten Island as part of his personal estate, thus beginning a tradition of Manhattan land-grabbing that continues to today.

However, Van Twiller's greed, like many present-day mogul's, was his downfall. The Dutch government became alarmed and he was recalled in 1638. The fortunes of New Netherlands slowly declined, its resources drained by constant wars with the Indians. The British took advantage of the bankruptcy of the West India Company and con-quered the settlement when it was at its weakest. They renamed the colony "New York" in 1664 in honor of the Duke of York.

First under Dutch rule, then as a British colony, the small town that had begun as a waterfront adjunct to Van Twiller's Bossen Bouwerie grew. Originally called "Green Village," it came to be known as Greenwich Village and was connected to the main New York City colony at the southern end of the island by a single road, Greenwich Road (now Greenwich Street) along the banks of the Hudson (landfill has since been added so that now Greenwich Street is several blocks from the river). During its years of British rule, Greenwich Village was a small community with commercial buildings near the river and country homes further east. In 1733 Sir Peter Warren bought the old Bossen Bouwerie and made it a luxurious country estate.

The continued growth in the Village's population and prosperity was due to a series of epidemics in lower New York. In 1739 a smallpox plague drove a number of wealthy families to buy homes in the highlands of Greenwich Village. Then a succession of yellow-fever plagues, from 1798 to 1822, brought even more families north, this

2

time to the Washington Square area. During the epidemics, authorities forced evacuation of the whole city and erected barricades along Chambers Street to prevent the return of the people. Only watchmen remained below it to guard property. Greenwich Village became the center of the metropolis as stores, banks, and other businesses moved north. The poorer families from the City migrated toward the west side of the Village.

In 1806, the Common Council of New York appointed a commission to begin the first of many efforts to make the Village conform to the physical pattern of New York. They leveled the hills and high points of the area. When the gridiron pattern, to which all the City's streets above 14th Street now conform, was laid out, the City realized the impossibility of razing all the buildings that lined the Village's winding streets. So the little streets have remained, helping to create the atmosphere that makes the Village a community distinct from the rest of the City.

As the City moved north, the Village became a backwater, and eventually new immigrants arrived. First came the Irish in the 1850s. Then, after the Civil War, African-Americans began to settle in the southeast Village, and, in the 1890s, the Italian immigrants arrived. The population of the Village grew swiftly, changing considerably in its ethnic and economic composition. East of Washington Square and west of Sixth Avenue, the old-line aristocrats quickly moved north to avoid the advancing line of immigrants and low-income minorities. By the turn of the century, Greenwich Village was largely a low-rent area inhabited predominantly by an Irish, African-American, and Italian population.

About 1910, artists and writers who came to New York discovered the low rents in Greenwich Village. The area's urban charms, similar to the Left Bank district of Paris, were as persuasive as the rents. And so the "Bohemians" arrived. Their Bohemianism was real, not pretended, as historian Albert Parry points out in *Garrets and Pretenders:*

> The Village was a state of mind helped along by certain adverse economic conditions . . . those Bohemians were our society's marginal men and women. While waiting for the public to recognize their talents, writers, artists, dancers, actors, directors refused to forsake their media, declined humdrum jobs and banded together in a Bohemia to make a gay virtue of their poverty.

A landmark sculptor's studio at 10th Street and Greenwich Avenue being demolished

In the tabloids of the day, the Village was pictured as a reservation set aside for Bohemians who frequented such rendezvous as Polly Holliday's Polly, Edith Unger's Mad Hatter, Mary Alletta Crump's Crumperie Tea Room, Charlie Read's Purple Pup, Tom Wallace's Golden Swan, Marie Marchard's Romany Marie, Sam Swart's TNT, Vera Black's Black Parrot on Sheridan Square, and Don Dickerman's Pirate's Den. Dickerman's place excelled over the competition as a tourist attraction with an atmosphere of lawless pleasure. The Pirate's Den had a coffin as a signboard, and patrons entered this basement fantasyland by crossing a gangplank under a Jolly Roger that flew over the hatchway. The club's murky interior was lighted by flickering ship lanterns, with ropes, tackle, cobwebs, cannons, and shrieking parrots adding to the atmosphere. Drinks like "Black Skull Punch" could be ordered from waiters dressed as buccaneers. The Pirate's Band, which played from a lifeboat suspended from the ceiling, entertained the customers. The house staff obliged customers by staging periodic brawls with flashing cutlasses and mock pistol fire. Dickerman

4

himself was in costume as a swashbuckling pirate, complete with an eyepatch and golden earring.

Greenwich Village quickly became known as the "cradle of the counterculture," a saleable slogan exploited by the tea rooms, bars, and restaurants, suggesting that famous characters were their patrons and could be seen at their establishments. Basement clubs sprang up where "poets" recited their verses by candlelight, and gullible tourists (just like in the 1950s) flocked in to absorb art and culture. These places made the candle-stuffed-in-the-Chianti-bottle a Village symbol.

These dimly lit, arty dens helped to carry the Village's reputation as an intellectual, artistic, Bohemian arena. It also became known for Free Love, Free Speech, Radicalism, Marxism, Trotskyism, Leninism, Socialism, and bizarre forms of sexual eccentricity. Greenwich Village was running wild—all-night parties, boys walking the streets in pajamas, girls smoking in the streets, everybody drinking and living from moment to moment. Caroline R. Ware in *Greenwich Village 1920–1930* tells how

> more adventurous young people were attracted to the Village by the lure of the excitement and daring of Bohemian life, and especially by the opportunity of sex experience and experiment. This new phase corresponded with the burst of "flaming youth" which made the elders' hair rise on end in the mid-twenties.

Greenwich Village's fabled tolerance of sexual experimentation made it a beacon for what the tabloids obliquely termed "the Third Sex." The Village harbored a disproportionate share of gay and lesbian households as well as gay "personality" clubs, tea rooms, speakeasies, and rental halls for drag balls. Although run with discretion, these establishments were part of the spectacle that lured tourists to the neighborhood. Several bathhouses advertised their services euphemistically as "exclusively for gentlemen." Because eccentric dress and unconventional gender behavior were keynotes of Bohemian culture, gay couples enjoyed considerable latitude in their lifestyle, passing as "normal" nonconformists. Prone to wearing male attire, jane heap and Margaret Anderson, lovers and editors of the progressive *Little Review,* held a salon that drew many prominent lesbians and gays from the local art community.

5

East 10th Street in the 1950s

Greenwich Village also exerted a powerful influence on the American literary imagination. By the 1920s, Bohemians had become legendary characters through the novels of writers who had firsthand knowledge of the Village counterculture, as well as through numerous little magazines. Dozens of radical magazines appeared in the prewar Village as vehicles of expression for new ideas and literary forms. These were known as "little" magazines not because they were small in format but rather as a reflection of their restricted production budgets and limited circulation. Refusing to make concessions to popular taste, these periodicals adopted an irreverent posture toward the conventions of rhyme, punctuation, language, illustration, and subject matter that commercial publishers had long avoided. Much of this transferred years later to the unruly, undisciplined writing of the Beat Generation.

Among these magazines was *The Little Review*, a sponsor of experimental fiction and poetry. Its pioneering serialization of James Joyce's *Ulysses*, beginning in the March 1918 issue, led to the editors' conviction on charges of pandering obscenity. Four "offending" *Ulysses* installments were destroyed by the U.S. Post Office. *The Seven*

Arts, edited by James Oppenheim, Waldo Frank, and Van Wyck Brooks, was founded with the ambitious goal of spearheading a modern American literary renaissance. Its contents reflected cultural criticism, Pacifism, and Freudianism. *Seven Arts's* opposition to the First World War led to the magazine's financial collapse.

Playboy: A Portfolio of Art & Satire, published until 1923, was less politically controversial and more aesthetically oriented than some of the other little magazines. It originated from The Washington Square Book Shop at 17 West 8th Street and listed among its "sponsors" D. H. Lawrence, Walt Whitman, Friedrich Nietzsche, Jesus Christ, and William Blake. *Others: An Anthology of New Verse* first appeared in 1915 under the editorship of Alfred Kreymborg, an imagist poet. In spite of only 300 paid subscribers, *Others* published the work of Wallace Stevens, T. S. Eliot, Conrad Aiken, Maxwell Bodenheim, Marianne Moore, William Carlos Williams, Charles Demuth, Maurice Prendergast, and William Zorach. Other noteworthy journals included *The Ink Pot,* published out of Sheridan Square, which was devoted to promoting the unique spirit of the Bohemian Village, and *The Masses,* a left-wing monthly that attracted the best writing and artistic talent of the day.

Aside from the "little" magazines for the intellectuals and real Bohemians, there was a whole new industry emerging to accommodate the ever-growing tourist market. There were postcards, portfolios of Village etchings, and dozens of guidebooks (like this one!) dedicated specifically to the swinging Latin Quarter. Anna Chapin's 1917 landmark study *Greenwich Village* was bound in leather for tourists. Greenwich Village became a paying proposition for nearly everyone.

The most famous Village entrepreneur was Guido Bruno, a self-styled Bohemian who rented an attic room at 58 Washington Square and plastered it with huge signs proclaiming that Bruno's Garret was the headquarters of art and inspired genius. He collected his freaks and called them "talent" that he discovered and nurtured, and he charged a modest entrance admission to tourists who wished to see them. Women admirers paid him to publish their verse and stories in book form; few of these "books" ever appeared. With his windfalls, he did publish a number of little, off-beat magazines, *Bruno's Bohemia, Bruno's Weekly,* and others, collector's items that can sometimes be found in antiquarian bookstores.

The realtors discovered the Villagers too, and welcomed the peculiar ones to uphold the fame of the Village, including oddballs like "Doris The Dope" who became famous after she took a nude moonlit bath in the Washington Square fountain. She claimed she was abandoned by a titled lord. "She coughed for a living," as Albert Parry points out. "The bourgeois slummers were impressed that she was in the last stages of consumption and gave her money. On reaching a set sum, she would stop coughing and retreat to the Brevoort [Hotel] in her best clothes as jubilant as the writers and artists who came there with their editors' checks."

One of the more surreal characters to surface in the Village during the war years was the Baroness Elsa von Freytag von Loring-hoven. A mysterious woman, she had recently separated from her rich husband to pursue a career as a Cubist painter and Dadaist poet in the Village. Although the Baroness did publish work and posed as a life model for local artists, her primary vocation was that of high priestess of freedom of dress and behavior to the Bohemian cult. Margaret Anderson, of *The Little Review*, published her verses, and declared the Baroness to be "the only figure of our generation who deserves the epithet extraordinary." Lloyd Morris in his 1951 book *Incredible New York* describes the Baroness in this way:

> Penniless, often starving, she lived in two tenement rooms with three dogs, painting and writing verse and parading the Village streets in eccentric costumes which frequently caused her to be arrested. Once she shaved her head and lacquered it bright vermilion. To a benefit concert for *The Little Review* held at the Provincetown Playhouse, she came attired in a trailing blue-green dress, carrying a peacock-feather fan, her face powdered yellow, her lips painted black, a canceled postage stamp affixed to one cheek, and wearing, for a hat, an inverted coal-scuttle. Introduced to the singer who had performed, the Baroness asked her why she sang. "I sing for humanity," the singer replied. Contemptuously, the Baroness boomed out, "I wouldn't lift a leg for humanity."

The invasion of sightseers into the Village searching for bizarre characters was deplored by most residents who valued the seclusion this quaint backwater provided from the City's hustle and bustle. Committed

8th Street looking east from Sixth Avenue in 1950

radicals abhorred the carnival mood and shuddered to encounter bourgeois interlopers in their favorite hideaways. Realtors, merchants, movie makers, bus lines, and theater companies exploited the economic bonanza of the community's spiraling Latin Quarter allure. They proceeded to farm "Bohemianism" as a cash crop. By the 1920s, realty signs were ubiquitous on Village properties. Much-hated plutocratic Washington Square landlord, Vincent Pepe, was at the forefront, buying up tenements and row houses and quadrupling the rent by adding partitions, fresh paint, and upgraded plumbing to his properties. His restorative touch is said to have triggered a gentrification campaign

9

that resulted in a 140 percent increase in local rents between 1920 and 1930. Some rents skyrocketed to twenty-nine dollars a month according to the 1930 census.

After the Second World War, the Village became home to an important new movement: The "New York" school of painters. Diverse artists such as Willem de Kooning, Milton Resnick, Joan Mitchell, William Littlefield, and many others found inexpensive loft space in the then-unexplored neighborhood of the East Village. They were followed by musicians, poets, and writers. Some of the more experimental of the authors—including Allen Ginsberg and Jack Kerouac—became leaders in the fledgling Beat movement, which came to full flower in the late '50s.

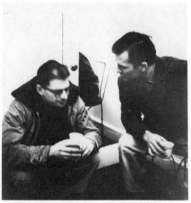

Allen Ginsberg and Jack Kerouac at a Hansa Gallery opening, March 16, 1960

In the 1960s, the Village became a center of social protest and change. The folk clubs nurtured new talents, including a young guitar-strumming songwriter named Bob Dylan. Washington Square Park continued to be a center for rallies and protest marches, as well as a gathering place for guitar players, hippies, the down-and-out, and the up-and-coming despite the fact that it was against the law in the early '60s to play an instrument or read poetry in the park. As the '60s wore on, the antiwar and Civil Rights movements came onto the Village stage.

In the 1970s, the gay and women's liberation movements entered the Village scene. The Stonewall Riots marked the beginning of expanded consciousness of gay rights, and the Village, long tolerant of homosexual lifestyles, became a focal point for gays worldwide in their struggle for acceptance. Many prominent women's liberation movement leaders called the Village their home, and they held marches and rallies throughout the neighborhood.

The 1980s and 1990s have seen further changes in the Village landscape. Yuppification, the invasion of well-heeled urban dwellers, has driven Village prices even higher. The traditional Bohemian Village has experienced dramatic changes: the loss of fine old landmarks, the rise of luxury apartment houses, soaring rents, urban renewal, and a population shift that began in the 1970s to the East Village and Soho and in the 1980s to Tribeca. 1930's twenty-nine-dollar-a-month rent for a railroad flat is now $800, and the Village of the '90s boasts some of the highest rents in the city.

As time passes, people still come and pay whatever the price may be to be part of the Greenwich Village experience. Some newcomers want to relive its history, to imagine that they see Jimi Hendrix strolling on 8th Street, to watch Janis Joplin chug-a-lug a bottle of Southern Comfort, to hear Abbie Hoffman beating his antiwar drums,

Spectators at a gay pride celebration

or to hear Jack Kerouac read a poem to jazz. Some even come to pay homage to Jimmy Walker, Edna St. Vincent Millay, John Reed, Mabel Dodge, Eugene O'Neill, Joe Gould, and Ida Tarbell.

Others come to play a different role, to become a part of Village history for the next generation of the avant garde. The Village has seen it all: the search for artistic innovation and personal freedom that began in the Flapper days of the Lost Generation, the anguished philosophy espoused by the post-World-War-II Existentialists, the self-seeking inwardness of the early '50s Silent Generation, the unconventional lifestyles of the Beats, the carefree '60s flower power that characterized the Hippies, the anarchy of the Yippies, the self-seeking Yuppies of the '80s, and the neo-conservatives of the '90s. And therein lies the secret of the Village's everlasting appeal—its amazing tolerance of people so diverse that their only point of agreement is the necessity for the existence of their community, Greenwich Village.

Washington Square

Washington Square Park; Washington Square Arch; Statues in the Park;
The Fountain; Washington Square North; Washington Square West;
Washington Square South; Judson Memorial Church; New York University;
Washington Place; Triangle Shirtwaist Fire/Brown Building

The focal point of Greenwich Village is **Washington Square**, a park
lying at the foot of Fifth Avenue. Whether it is spring or summer,
autumn or winter, throngs of Villagers and visitors alike converge on
the Square . . . on foot, on rollerblades, bicycles, and motor scooters,
in taxis, in sight-seeing buses. Mothers and fathers with babies, artists
and intellectuals, bankers and ex-Beatniks, ex-Hippies, Zen Bud-
dhists, swamis, shoe clerks, poets, writers, and musicians all gather
here. Part of the day-to-day festival that makes Greenwich Village a
community apart from all others can be seen in Washington Square.

Originally marshland, the eight-acre parcel was purchased by the
City for use as a potter's field (or graveyard). An ancient work entitled
The Malignant Fever in New York records the burial of 667 victims of
the 1797 yellow-fever epidemic in the graveyard. In August 1965, a
Con Ed excavation in the northeast corner of the park uncovered a
sealed underground room containing twenty-five skeletons, possibly
yellow-fever victims isolated after death. The park also served as the
City's public hanging ground. According to legend, the Marquis de
Lafayette witnessed the mass hanging of twenty highwaymen there.

Washington Square Park looking south from the top of the Arch, during NYU graduation exercises, May 1992

The last recorded hanging was in 1822 when a female murderer was executed.

In 1826, the area was rehabilitated as a parade ground, which proved impractical when the heavy artillery on display sometimes caved into the graves below. The Square was then reconfigured as an airy commons, complete with a fountain and intersecting pedestrian paths. It was already described as a most fashionable residential neighborhood in an 1828 guide to the City. Two years later, new town houses were built in the Greek Revival style along the north side of the Square.

A wood-and-plaster arch, straddling Fifth Avenue, was erected in 1889 as part of the festivities marking the centennial of George Washington's inauguration as the first president of the U.S. The imposing structure so took the fancy of the public that a fundraising campaign resulted in the construction of a marble monument, **Washington Arch**, in 1895. It was placed several yards below the original arch to serve as a gateway to the park. Designed by Stanford White, the most celebrated architect of his day, the arch has a bas relief by Frederick MacMonnies and is flanked by two statues of Washington, both of which, after nearly eighty years, are visibly eroded by pollution. The sculpture on the western pedestal, "Washington in Peace," was executed and added in 1918 by A. Sterling Calder, father of Alexander Calder. The sculpture on the eastern pedestal, "Washington in War," was executed in 1916 by Hermon A. MacNeil.

The arch is eighty-six feet high and thirty feet wide and was considered by its creator to be the greatest arch in the world. Aside from being the subject of enough paintings to fill the Louvre, the Arch, in the winter of 1916, was the scene of a quaint and unusual revolution commonly called the "Washington Square Picnic." Gertrude Drick, nicknamed the "Golden Bird," invited Marcel Duchamp, John Sloan, Forrest Mann, Charles Ellis, and Betty Turner to the top of the Arch. Entering through the iron door at the base, armed with hot-water bottles to sit on, Chinese lanterns, red balloons, food, and drink, they climbed the 110 steps to the top where each guest was handed a loaded cap pistol. They read poems, fired the cap pistols, and Sloan declared Greenwich Village a "Free Republic, Independent of Uptown." This event has been immortalized in a John Sloan etching called the *Arch-Conspirators*.

14

The Fountain, directly in the center of the park, is 100 feet in diameter and was installed in 1871. The pedestals surrounding the fountain may have been intended at one time for sculpture. Today, they function mostly as vantage points for photographers and sunbathers. The fountain *is* the heart of the Village; here, on a summer Sunday, Villagers gather to pick guitars, take photographs, sunbathe, meditate, make a speech, walk the dog, write poetry, shoot movies, meet friends, or catch an impromptu performance. All that is missing is a community bulletin board.

The present layout of the park was established in 1870. Reminiscent of that era are the meandering walkways, wooden benches, and a dozen wide entrances. At the southwest corner of the park are a number of chess and checkerboard tables that are in constant use, providing recreation for older, more sedentary players. In addition, the park serves a variety of community needs. There are the children's playgrounds, with a protocol all their own, that are heavily

Folk dancing in Washington Square Park, July 1951

patronized on weekdays. In springtime, tulips and pansies are planted by the Parks Department; in the summer, when the city is drenched with sun, the authorities turn on the multi-unit sprinkler and droves of children splash with delight in the chilly water of the fountain. And, during August, a local civic association sponsors a series of outdoor chamber-music concerts.

Two statues stand silently in the park. On the eastern side is a bronze monument of the Italian patriot Giuseppe Garibaldi sculpted by Giovanni Turini and erected in 1888 as a gift to the Italians of New York. On the west side is a bronze bust by J. Q. A. Ward of Alexander Lyman Holley who developed the Bessemer process for the manufacture of steel in the U.S. Less well-known is the forty-five-foot flagpole commemorating the veterans of the First World War.

Washington Square North (Fifth Avenue east to University Place), the old row of red-brick and limestone houses, was designated by the New York City Landmarks Commission as "the most important and imposing block front of early 19th century town houses in the city." Enhanced by its location on the square, the Greek Revival row is a model of community planning that still has an aura of fashionable privacy imparted by its unique and continuous iron railing along the sidewalk.

This block was owned by Sailors' Snug Harbor, who leased the property for residential development. Martin E. Thompson designed the row, which was built in 1832–33 to house the most socially prominent New Yorkers of the era. John Johnston, one of the early leaders in the movement to develop the land, built the largest house on the block at number 7 for his residence. His son, John Taylor Johnston, was the first president of the Metropolitan Museum of Art. Johnston's business partner, James Boorman, built and occupied number 13, the corner house. Number 8 was once the official residence of the City's mayor. Number 12 was also used as a mayoral residence when it was occupied from 1879 to 1905 by Edward Cooper, a fusion mayor (endorsed by all parties) who was the son of the founder of Cooper Union. Authors Henry James, Edith Wharton, and William Dean Howells all lived and worked in number 1.

In more recent times, as the Village became home to artists and writers rather than merchants and bankers, number 3 gained fame as the residence of John Dos Passos, who lived here while writing *Manhattan Transfer,* and such well-known artists as Rockwell Kent, Walter Pach, Frederick Stokes (who accompanied Admiral Robert Edwin Peary on his Arctic explorations), and Edward Hopper.

Washington Square West, the continuation of MacDougal Street, is a mixture of somewhat nondescript apartment houses and the NYU Hayden Residence Hall, formerly the Hotel Holley, at number 33. A nostalgic note survives in a fountain, a statuette of Pan by Gutzon Borglum, set into a wall in a dining room. The fountain formerly was fed by an underground stream called Minetta Brook, which the original Village inhabitants called Minetta Water, and which flowed above ground through Washington Square and nearby Minetta Lane. When the University acquired the property, the brook water feeding the fountain was disconnected and replaced with tap water from the building's plumbing system. A plaque above the fountain reads "Flowing under Greenwich Village 'till memory has made it a legend, the waters of Minetta again greet the light through this fountain as the spirit of Manhattan rising to greater glory." To the chagrin of contractors and architects, the brook still zigzags its way under the Village streets, and workers excavating the nearby Loeb Student Center and School of Law found themselves knee deep in Minetta water.

Folksingers Paul Prestopino and Winnie Winston in Washington Square Park, July 26, 1959

Eleanor Roosevelt, wife of President Franklin Delano Roosevelt, took an apartment at 29 Washington Square West in 1942, where the Roosevelts intended to retire when the president's third term ended in 1944. However, he won an unprecedented fourth term, and then died in office on April 12, 1945. Mrs. Roosevelt kept the apartment until 1949, and she was frequently seen strolling in the park with Fala, their black scottie. Today a plaque on the building commemorates her stay there.

A humanitarian, reformer, and stateswoman, Mrs. Roosevelt was the author of several books as well as a widely syndicated newspaper column called "My Day" that she also read over the radio. Her distinctively high-pitched voice and measured enunciation became known throughout the world. Mrs. Roosevelt's involvement in politics began after her husband's crippling illness from polio in 1921, and she proved herself an invaluable adviser on social welfare after he became president. In 1941 she became assistant director of the Office of Civilian Defense. After FDR's death she extended her activities, first as a delegate to the United Nations Assembly in 1946, then as chair of the U.N. Human Rights Commission, and finally as U.S. representative to the U.N.'s General Assembly.

With the exception of Judson Memorial Church, **Washington Square South** is lined with NYU buildings. Vanderbilt Hall, the law school at MacDougal Street, is modeled after the English Inns of Court. The Hagop Kevorkian Center for Near Eastern Studies and the Judson Residence Hall share the same block; the Catholic Center and Loeb Student Center are on the next block. The Elmer Holmes Bobst Library is at the corner of La Guardia Place.

Before these buildings were put up, Washington Square South was lined with single-family pre–Civil War town houses. Some were converted into boardinghouses. The most celebrated of the inexpensive boarding hotels along Washington Square South was number 61, managed by Madame Katarina Branchard. Author Albert Parry remembers the house as rickety, ratty, and unsanitary. This Swiss-born landlady mothered several generations of struggling Village painters, journalists, dramatists, and authors creating a *de facto* arts colony in the process. Among those who found shelter and stimulating company there were the writers Frank Norris, Stephen Crane, O. Henry, the opera singer Adelina Patti, and the poet Alan Seeger. This roster of creative lodgers earned the address acclaim as the "House of Genius." After Madame Branchard's death at eighty-one in 1937, her son continued to live in the old boardinghouse until it was torn down in 1948.

In 1906, Willa Cather took a studio at 60 Washington Square South, where Edith Lewis, who was to be her lifetime friend, also had a room. (The numbers run consecutively as they do on Washington Square North). "In 1906," Lewis wrote in her biography *Willa Cather Living,* "Washington Square was one of the most charming places in New York."

The threadbare row house at number 42 Washington Square South was another popular port for young artists and writers newly transported to the Village. This particular boardinghouse came to function as a makeshift alumni club for Ivy League intellectuals drifting into the neighborhood. John Reed, fresh out of Harvard and eager to write poetry, found lodgings there in 1911. His experiences as a roomer inspired a volume of verse, *The Day in Bohemia: Or, Life Among the Artists,* privately printed in 1913. Begun on stationery pilfered from the Café Lafayette, the poem described the frivolity and rugged conditions of life in the barracks at number 42. Dubbing the place "Parnassus Flats," Reed saluted his fellow inmates as "inglorious Miltons by the score and Rodins, one to every floor." The poems were dedicated to journalist Lincoln Steffens, Reed's mentor and fellow boardinghouse tenant.

Judson Memorial Church is at 55 Washington Square South (at Thompson Street). Built of amber brick with a Lombard campanile (bell tower) designed by Stanford White and an adjoining five-story apartment house, the church has twelve stained-glass windows

Judson Memorial Church

executed by John LaFarge. It was built by Dr. Edward Judson in 1888 to honor his father, the Rev. Adoniram Judson, who was the first American missionary to serve overseas. The apartment house and tower were eventually sold to New York University, but the church has remained an active force in the community. Since the 1950s, it has been the center of much avant-garde artistic activity, inspired by its esteemed minister, the Rev. Howard Moody. The clergyman has defended folksingers in Washington Square, assisted young drug addicts, helped poets confined in jail, and is perhaps one of the few clergymen whose parishioners address him by his first name. Since the late '50s, the church has been host to political conferences, dance concerts, poetry readings, art exhibits, concerts, and performance pieces by such artists as Claes Oldenburg, Jim Dine, Allan Kaprow, and Yoko Ono.

New York University occupies all the buildings on Washington Square East. It is New York's largest private university with six campuses and thirteen schools. The first president of New York University's governing council was Albert Gallatin, Secretary of the Treasury in Thomas Jefferson's cabinet. Gallatin and his cofounders hoped that the new university would be a "national university" that would provide a "rational and practical education for all."

Large numbers of students and faculty members live in the Village, a fact that has had a highly favorable impact on the social and cultural life of the area. For decades however, the school has engaged in a dialogue with Villagers who question the conversion of residential buildings into school buildings, thus making the Square, in effect, a downtown campus.

The University is nevertheless a community institution with a colorful history. It was incorporated in 1831 as an independent, nonsectarian institution with the revolutionary aim of providing the city with a college in which the offspring of "the artisan and the tradesman shall be as welcome as the children of the rich," and where practical as well as academic subjects would be taught.

As a measure of economy, the contractor building NYU planned to use stone cut by convicts in Sing Sing prison. When this news reached the Stone-Cutters Guild, the membership paraded through Washington Square in the first demonstration of organized labor in New York history. The historical significance of the occasion failed to move the University's officials. The 27th Regiment of the National Guard was summoned and the demonstrators were forced to withdraw after a four-day siege known historically as the Stone-Cutters Riot of October 24, 1833.

The university's **Gothic Tower,** which was the cause of this demonstration, became famous as laboratory and home for some of America's best-known scientists, inventors, and artists. For many years after its founding, the University was plagued by financial problems. As a solution, some of its classrooms were leased as laboratories and rented as lodgings. Among the Tower's distinguished tenants were inventor Samuel Colt; painters Winslow Homer, Eastman Johnson, and George Innes; poet Walt Whitman; and architect Richard Morris Hunt, few of whom had an official connection with the University. While living in the Gothic Tower during the 1830s, Colt invented his deadly revolver; working concurrently in the same building was Samuel F. B. Morse, who invented the telegraph, and NYU chemistry professor John William Draper, who made early experiments in the Daguerreotype process. In 1839, on the Tower's roof, Draper produced one of the first photographs of a human face ever taken in full sunlight. The Tower was replaced in 1894 by the present Main Building, which was, in its time, considered an architectural marvel.

20

Henry James was born in 1843 at 21 Washington Place in a house that stood on the corner of Mercer Street. He lived there only six months before his family took him to Europe. The family moved back to the Village in 1847, first to 11 Fifth Avenue, then to a town house at 57 West 14th Street. Both Henry and his philosopher brother

NYU Graduation, May 1992

William spent many hours at 19 Washington Square North with their grandmother Elizabeth Walsh. Henry wrote his most celebrated novel *Washington Square* while living in Greenwich Village, but lived much of his life in England and, in 1915, became a British subject.

In November 1945, Richard Wright, the author of *Native Son*, lived in a four-room apartment on the third floor of 82 Washington Place, the same building in which Willa Cather had lived thirty-five years earlier.

The site of the **Triangle Shirtwaist Fire** is memorialized by a bronze plaque mounted high on NYU's Brown Building at the northwest corner of Washington Place and Greene Street. This horrible tragedy took 146 lives, mostly poor Italian and Jewish women and young girls, on the afternoon of Saturday, March 25, 1911. (Gloria McDarrah's father, Louis Schoffel, an immigrant garment worker, was fired by the Triangle factory that same year before the fire took place.) Triangle occupied the upper three floors of the ten-story Brown building. The fire was fueled by flammable cloth scraps littered throughout the factory. Finding the exit doors bolted by management to deter employee theft and early departures from shifts, garment workers died in the smoky fire, and many more lost their lives leaping to the street below.

Appalling working conditions in these sweatshops were widely known, but pressure from influential businessmen kept city and state officials from enacting safety measures. A state commission appointed to investigate the fire was headed by Robert F. Wagner and Alfred E. Smith. The commission's three-volume report, issued in 1912, covered factory sanitation, fire hazards, occupational diseases, child labor, factory inspection, the employment of women, and safety. As a result of the investigation, state laws were enacted that reformed the fire code and prohibited crowding in all commercial buildings. The owners of the Triangle Company were indicted, but were later acquitted of responsibility for the deadly tragedy.

Lower Fifth Avenue

Lower Fifth Avenue Mansions; Mabel Dodge; Brevoort Hotel; Hotel Lafayette; O. Henry; Mark Twain; Thomas A. Edison; Washington Square Outdoor Art Exhibit; MacDougal Alley; Washington Mews; Pen and Brush Club; Church of the Ascension; First Presbyterian Church; Salmagundi Club; Benjamin N. Cardozo School of Law; *Forbes* Magazine Galleries; Parsons School of Design

By the middle of the 19th century, **Lower Fifth Avenue** beginning at Washington Square was the stronghold of many Knickerbocker (old Dutch) families. It was an avenue of dignified appearance with its brick and brownstone mansions, some of the earliest of which were built in the 1830s. Distinguished old Dutch families who lived on lower Fifth Avenue included the Rhinelanders, Howlands, Aspinwalls, Belmonts, and Minturns. Misses Julia and Serena Rhinelander lived for fifty years in a large Georgian house on the west side of the base of Fifth Avenue; it is now an apartment house. Their neighbors were the shipbuilding Howlands, including Gardiner Greene Howland and his brother Samuel Shaw, both homeowners in the neighborhood. Sam married the daughter of August Belmont, who lived at 82 Fifth Avenue, near 14th Street. The Howlands's business partner William Henry Aspinwall was another prominent Fifth Avenue dweller; he founded the Union League Club. Yet another Dutch shipbuilder, Robert Brown Minturn, lived at 64 Fifth Avenue; he was the founder of the Association for Improving Conditions of Poor and Incoming Foreigners.

Prominent Knickerbockers on lower Fifth Avenue were definitely among the rich and famous. John Cleve Green of 16 Fifth Avenue was prominent in the China trade and spent a great deal of time at sea. Social reformer Henry Bergh lived at 17 Fifth Avenue and organized the Society for the Prevention of Cruelty to Animals; he was the author of *Streets of New York*. His father, Christian Bergh, opened a shipyard on the East River in 1785.

A house near 9th Street, 23 Fifth Avenue, was owned by Daniel Edgar Sickles, a major general in the Civil War, where he lost his right leg. Prior to the War, Sickles shot and killed Philip Barton Key, son of Francis Scott Key, because of Key's "attentions" to Mrs. Sickles. He was acquitted on a "plea of temporary aberration." Sickles was a distinguished lawyer who was a prime mover behind the acquisition of Central Park for the City.

In the 1920s, 23 Fifth Avenue was the home of Edwin and **Mabel Dodge** and became the focus of Bohemian activity in the pre–World War I Village. Mrs. Dodge moved to New York after an extended stay abroad, and she devoted her considerable resources to establishing a salon where a cross-section of social classes and ideological camps gathered to discuss everything from Freud and birth control to Cubism and the labor movement. Her stunningly appointed all-white parlor included a white bearskin rug in front of a white marble fireplace. In addition to interesting conversation, her salon sometimes offered other types of stimulating fare, including a peyote-eating ceremony she staged once to enhance her "occult" powers.

Emma Goldman and John Reed were regulars at her salon, and such talented figures as Walter Lippmann, Jo Davidson, Lincoln Steffens, and Carl Van Vechten were frequent guests. Many Village intellectuals were introduced to the radical labor movement at the Dodge salon. The three organizers instrumental in the 1913 Paterson silk workers' strike—Elizabeth Gurley Flynn, Carlo Tresca, and IWW leader Bill Haywood—brought insights into the struggles of American labor to the salon. Though influential in its era, Mabel Dodge's salon was short-lived. She moved to Washington Square when she remarried, but could not repeat her earlier social success there, and soon moved to New Mexico.

At Fifth Avenue and 8th Street the 1950s Brevoort apartment building was built on the site of the old **Brevoort Hotel**, which was demolished in 1954. A distinguished artistic and social clientele frequented the old hotel, which had opened one hundred years earlier. The land was originally part of a farm owned by Henry Brevoort, whose name was given to the hotel. In 1902, French-born Raymond Orteig bought the hotel and gave it a Parisian flavor that attracted a tide of Bohemian customers. Its basement café became a customary destination for those with loose change to spend. Dinners to celebrate the sale of a book, play, or painting were reserved for the Brevoort café, as were the breakfast parties that traditionally followed all-night Village balls.

Another meeting place for Bohemian literati was the Hotel Lafayette on University Place at 9th Street. Its European-style café offered French food, good French wine, foreign newspapers, and a Paris bistro atmosphere that reminded the Bohemian crowd of their student days in Paris—although, according to one observer, the drinks were bad, costing twice as much as anyplace else, and the waiters were surly. Nevertheless, the Lafayette was the unrivaled meeting place of high Bohemia during the '20s. John Sloan immortalized the old marquee in a 1927 painting called *The Lafayette*. The café was closed in 1949; in its place is a nondescript apartment house with a restaurant on the street floor.

O. Henry (William Sydney Porter) lived for many years in a rooming house at 49 East 9th Street. His hall bedroom is described in his story *The Skylight Room*. The rooming house later became the headquarters of the *Villager* newspaper, which subsequently had to move to make way for a skyscraper. Although O. Henry became the best-known short-story writer in the world, he had served time in his youth in a federal penitentiary for absconding with funds from a Texas bank in which he had worked as a clerk. After his release in 1902, he came to New York and was perennially plagued by one or more blackmailers acquainted with his prison past. He died in 1910 of a liver ailment.

On the southeast corner of Fifth Avenue and 9th Street, adjoining the old Brevoort Hotel, stood 21 Fifth Avenue, where Samuel Clemens (better known as Mark Twain) lived from 1904 to 1908. Clemens moved there with his daughter, Jean, and his housekeeper after his wife's death. Despite efforts to establish it as a museum (the architect for the house was James Renwick, who had also designed Grace Church on 10th Street), it was torn down in 1954 to make way for the Brevoort apartment building.

The Washington Square Outdoor Art Show

Thomas Alva Edison occupied a mansion at 65 Fifth Avenue during the 1880s that he used as a home and an office. Edison's son Charles, a dilettante poet, later opened a phonograph and record store called the Edison Diamond Disc Shop in a town house at 10 Fifth Avenue that still stands at the northwest corner of 8th Street. Above the store, The Thimble Theatre, a collaborative venture of Village publisher Guido Bruno and the younger Edison, functioned as a free showcase for aspiring composers, musicians, playwrights, and poets to perform new works. In February 1916, the first American production of August Strindberg's *Miss Julie* was offered here. The partnership between Bruno and Edison terminated that same year due to artistic differences.

The **Washington Square Outdoor Art Exhibit** fills Village streets with crowds of weekend strollers every spring and fall. Actually, it is somewhat of a misnomer, since most of the exhibitors are no longer on Washington Square, but along University Place, La Guardia Place, and adjoining streets. When the art show was launched in 1932, its aim was to exhibit the work of local artists and help alleviate some of the financial hardships caused by the Depression. An outpouring of public interest turned it into a twice yearly outdoor art festival.

Some shows have included upward of 1,000 artists from all over the country displaying for sale thousands of oil paintings, photographs, watercolors, sketches, and handicraft works ranging from unique wedding rings and small sculpture to "portraits" on copper mounted on velvet and framed in imitation leather. Prospective exhibitors are required to submit slides to a jury for approval, and all exhibitors are automatically in competition for prizes that are awarded in arts-and-crafts categories. A complete tour of the exhibition would consume nearly as much time as a visit to the Metropolitan Museum, but some critics might say it would be far less rewarding.

MacDougal Alley and Washington Mews are two curious and colorful cobble-stoned thoroughfares that lie on either side of Fifth Avenue, half-a-block north of Washington Square. Both are lined with two-century-old, beautifully preserved two-story carriage houses that once belonged to mansions facing the Square. With the advent of the automobile in the early twentieth century, these little service alleys were no longer used as stable facilities. Artists in search of studios in the area were attracted to the little back streets, and soon stalls became picturesque bungalows, rooftops sprouted skylights, and pretty shades of paint transformed the alleys into quaint byways.

West of Fifth Avenue, **MacDougal Alley** opens off MacDougal Street, and was named for an early state senator, Alexander MacDougal. In the late 1910s a tea room known as the Jumble Shop occupied the MacDougal Street corner. At the rear of the alley, a large stable was converted into a studio for sculptor and art patron Gertrude Vanderbilt Whitney, and to-

8 MacDougal Alley

day forms part of the New York Studio School, fronting on West 8th Street.

Charles Sheeler, one of the artists who frequented Whitney's Studio Club and profited from her support, painted the Alley's distinctive low, brick carriage houses with their irregular roof lines in

27

a 1924 oil. The painting is notable as one of Sheeler's exploratory efforts in Precisionism, a hard-edged style bordering on geometric abstraction. MacDougal Alley, nicknamed "Art Alley de Luxe," was also home to painter Edwin W. Deming. The street has the last antique gas lamps in New York, although they are now powered by electricity. To maintain security in the quiet alley, high iron gates, locked at night, were added in the 1960s.

Studio buildings in Washington Mews

Washington Mews, east of Fifth Avenue and entered from Fifth or University Place, served as stables in the 1800s for such occupants of the town houses facing Washington Square North as Pierre Lorillard, Richard Morris Hunt, and John Taylor Johnston. As fashionable New Yorkers moved north and artists invaded Greenwich Village, Washington Mews stables were converted into studios. The architectural firm of Maynicke & Franke turned twelve stables into studios in 1916 and covered the brick facades with stucco, studded them with tiles, and painted the doors, giving the mews a Mediterranean feel. New York University's *La Maison Française* occupies the natural-brick corner building that remained unaltered after the 1916 conversion. Artists who have lived or worked in the mews include Edward Hopper, whose studio was at the rear of his home on 3 Washington Square North. Other notable painters who lodged there over the years were William Glackens, Guy Pène du Bois, and Ernest Lawson.

The French-born sculptor Gaston Lachaise came to the Village in 1912, first to MacDougal Alley as an apprentice to Henry Hudson Kitson, an eminent academic sculptor, and then as an assistant to sculptor Paul Manship, who by 1915 worked on Washington Mews. By the early 1920s, Lachaise had his own studio on Washington Place, later moving to larger quarters on Washington Mews. Nearby on Waverly Place was the studio of Everett Shinn, one of the "Eight" who formed the Ashcan School, a group of artists dedicated to portraying the gritty, realistic world of urban America. Shinn had arrived in the Village at the turn of the century.

The **Pen and Brush Club** at 16 East 10th Street (Fifth Avenue) dates back to 1893. Founded to promote intellectual camaraderie among women, it is the oldest professional women's organization in the U.S. Its members are writers, painters, craftspeople, sculptors, and musicians. The landmark 1848 brownstone town house that the club occupies was built for grocer Abraham Bininger as his home. The spacious drawing rooms are now galleries for exhibits and receptions, a library, and offices. The garden floor has a dining room, and the three upper floors are used as studios and apartments by members. Over the years, the club's roster has included such illustrious women as authors Pearl Buck, Dorothy Canfield Fisher, and Anne Morrow Lindbergh; Eleanor Roosevelt; and poet Marianne Moore. Ida Tarbell, whose articles for *McClure's* magazine exposing the Standard Oil Company catapulted her to fame as one of the country's most tenacious muckrakers, served as president of the Pen and Brush Club for almost thirty-five years. Among the various activities held at Pen and Brush are art exhibits, writing workshops, arts-and-crafts classes, educational lectures, and films, concerts, and teas.

The **Church of the Ascension,** at the northwest corner of Fifth Avenue and 10th Street, was the first church to be built on the Avenue and was consecrated in 1841. The handsome English Gothic structure was designed by Richard Upjohn; Stanford White redecorated the interior in 1888. Behind the altar is a mural, *The Ascension of Our Lord* by John LaFarge, who also designed some of the beautiful stained-glass windows. Among the church's distinctive architectural features is the fine square tower that displays a triple-arched window above the Gothic pointed-arch doorway. The rectory adjoining the church on West 10th Street is also in Gothic Revival style, and the two form a harmonious composition. Through the year the church sponsors exceptionally fine concerts of religious music that are open to the public.

The church came into national prominence in June 1844 when it was the scene of a White House elopement, the only one in U.S. history. John Tyler secretly married his second wife, Julia Gardiner, thirty years his junior, there. After the service, the couple left the church in an open barouche drawn by four horses, and the secret was out.

The **First Presbyterian Church,** Fifth Avenue and 11th Street, is set back from the street behind an iron fence and a green front lawn and shrubs. The church and its adjoining church house occupy the

Edward Hopper in his Washington Mews studio, March 1, 1962

entire block front from 11th to 12th Streets. An outstanding example of early Gothic Revival architecture, it was designed by English-born architect Joseph Wells, and is modeled after the Church of St. Saviour in Bath. The cornerstone was laid in 1844 and the church opened for worship in 1846. This is one of the oldest Presbyterian congregations in Manhattan; it was formed in 1719. In its former location downtown, the church was notable for furnishing the Bible used by George Washington when he took the oath of office as president. The church house is a 20th-century addition, but its style conforms in material (brownstone) and design to the picturesque Gothic Revival church.

The **Salmagundi Club**, at 47 Fifth Avenue, was founded in 1871 for "the promotion of social intercourse among artists and the advancement of art." The name of the club derives from the early 19th-century periodical *The Salmagundi Papers,* which was published by Washington Irving "simply to instruct the young, reform the old, correct the town and castigate the aged." One of the few remaining town houses that once lined Fifth Avenue and one of the first to have a facade made entirely of brownstone, this grand mansion in the early Italianate style was built in 1852–53 for Irad Hawley, president of the Pennsylvania Coal Company.

The imposing entrance is richly framed with the original stone ornament. The first-floor rooms, lavishly decorated with carved marble chimney pieces and rosewood doors, have been carefully preserved by the club, which purchased the building in 1917. The roster of club members includes such distinguished names as artist John LaFarge, illustrator Howard Pyle, architect Stanford White, and stained-glass designer Louis C. Tiffany. From time to time, The Salmagundi Club sponsors invitational art exhibits that are open to the public.

The **Benjamin N. Cardozo School of Law**, established in 1976, sits at 55 Fifth Avenue in Yeshiva University's Brookdale Center. The school, named to honor the distinguished Associate Justice of the U.S. Supreme Court, prepares students for the professional practice of law and offers innovative courses of study within a traditional legal framework. Part of Yeshiva University, the nation's oldest and largest university under Jewish auspices, Cardozo has distinguished itself with broad-ranging programs such as the Bet Tzedek Legal Services Clinic, the Samuel and Ronnie Heyman Center on Corporate Governance, and the Leonard and Bea Diener Institute of Jewish Law, among others.

31

The *Forbes* Magazine Galleries on the ground floor of the Forbes Building at 62 Fifth Avenue (at 12th Street) are a tribute to the late owner and publisher Malcolm Forbes's passion for collecting. Forbes believed that "collectibles are not inanimate objects but are stimuli for the imagination" and these galleries certainly are stimulating. Permanent displays and changing exhibitions make up this tribute to Forbes's appreciation of collectibles. His fascination with the sea is reflected in the display of eight gold ground-glass panels designed by Jean Dupas for the Grand Saloon of the *Normandie,* one of the world's greatest ocean liners (that capsized at New York's Pier 88 on February 9, 1942), and a selection of over 500 toy boats. His interest in the military is evident in a series of dioramas and historical vignettes featuring over 12,000 toy soldiers (from his collection of over 100,000 military miniatures).

The Trophy Section, called the "Mortality of Immortality," evokes the inglorious descent of objects from priceless prize to flea-market find. Trophies run the gamut from the much-coveted prize for best chicken at the Northhampton Egg Laying Trials to the

The Rolling Stones in an impromptu performance on lower Fifth Avenue, May 1, 1975

urn that once held the ashes of Marion Hanbury Stewart. The American presidents exhibit, focusing on their personalities and problems, is a rotating selection culled from the magazine's 3,000 historical documents.

The most famous exhibits are the twelve Easter eggs made under the direction of jeweler/goldsmith Peter Carl Fabergé for the last two Czars of Russia at the turn of the century. These treasures, "never failing to stimulate one's appreciation for true beauty," as Forbes once wrote, comprise the largest private collection of Fabergé objects in the world. Finally, in the largest gallery, are changing exhibitions of paintings, photography, and other art from the Forbes's collection.

Since its founding in 1896 by William Merritt Chase, **Parsons School of Design**, 2 West 13th Street (at Fifth Avenue), has been a major force in art and design. The school has also contributed immeasurably to the formation of the concepts that underlie contemporary education in the visual arts. One of the major reasons for Parsons's impact on the world of art and design is its philosophy to enlist as faculty the best artists, designers, and photographers living and working in New York City. Programs are relevant and meaningful in terms of today's job market. Courses are offered in interior design, fashion, fine arts, floral and textile design, illustration, graphic and advertising design, and photography.

Village Square/8th Street/ Greenwich Avenue

Eighth Street; The Whitney Museum of American Art; Cedar Street Tavern; *The Little Review;* Sixth Avenue; Balducci's; Jefferson Market Court House; Spanish-Portuguese Cemetery; Patchin Place; Schapira Coffee Company; Milligan Place; The New School for Social Research; *The Dial;* Lesbian and Gay Community Services Center; Anaïs Nin; *The Masses;* Village Vanguard; Chicago B.L.U.E.S.; Eagle Tavern

Eighth Street stretching east from Sixth Avenue past University Place is a shopping center and main street of Greenwich Village. The street is alive with people from all over New York. Here the Villager or visitor can buy a designer dress, a piece of handmade jewelry, a bag of groceries, a box of books, see a film, or just stroll and window shop. At night, clubs like the Feenjon at 40 East 8th Street come alive with music and entertainment.

Eighth Street became a popular Village thoroughfare in the late 1940s after World War II when the main tourist attractions were Bon Soir, a sophisticated nightclub at 40 West 8th Street, Mary's, a gay bar at 55 West 8th Street, and a famous "whoopee parlor" at 52 West 8th Street called The Village Barn. Guests danced to hillbilly tunes beneath milk-pail chandeliers and ordered refreshments from yokels dressed in red-checkered shirts. In a loft located above this club was

Hans Hofmann in his 8th Street studio, February 27, 1960

the studio of the famous art teacher Hans Hofmann, who taught many of the second generation of New York artists at his Provincetown School. In 1970, 52 West 8th Street became famous as the recording studio of Jimi Hendrix, called Electric Lady. Hendrix's twenty-four track mixing console from the studio was recently sold at a Sotheby's auction.

Much of the pizzazz has left 8th Street because of the very high rents that force storekeepers to cater to transients; many of the arts-and-crafts stores have left. There is an amazing variety of retail stores on the street, including twenty-six shoe stores, seven jewelry stores, ten leather goods shops, four T-shirt/souvenir places, at least twelve clothing shops, and a large assortment of florists, dry cleaners, beauty parlors, sandwich and barbecue pits, travel agencies, palm readers, and eyeglass stores—all on two blocks!

But 8th Street also has great historical significance. The imposing seventy-five-foot-long building currently occupied by The New York Studio School at 8 West 8th Street is the former home of **The Whitney Museum of American Art**. It was built in 1838 as three private residences; in 1931, they were joined together to form one building. Although its facade looks a little seedy today, covered with graffiti, its prominent neoclassic doorway, huge arched windows, and inscription and stylized eagle above the doorway are all reminders of the building's past glory. The museum was located here for almost twenty-five years before it moved uptown to larger quarters.

The heiress to a great family fortune, Gertrude Vanderbilt Whitney (Mrs. Harry Payne Whitney) was the wealthy great-granddaughter of shipping and railroad magnate Cornelius Vanderbilt. She surprised her society friends by electing to lead an independent Bohemian life as a sculptor in Greenwich Village. In 1907 she took a studio in a remodeled stable on MacDougal Alley behind 8 West 8th Street and successfully integrated herself into the art community.

Although her own sculptural style was conservative, she welcomed all artists into her atelier, which, in 1916, became the Whitney Studio Club. Because she had lots of money, she was able to buy the art that she believed in, which became the nucleus of the Whitney Museum's collection.

The artists she exhibited and whose work she collected became the leading figures in American art of the period: Arthur B. Davies, Robert Henri, George Luks, Maurice Prendergast, Ernest Lawson, Everett Shinn, John Sloan, Stuart Davis, Edward Hopper, Joseph Stella, William J. Glackens, Reuben Nakian, Reginald Marsh, Walt

Jimi Hendrix in Electric Lady Studio with Eddie Kramer (l) and Jim Marron (r), June 16, 1970

Kuhn, Guy Pène du Bois, Charles Demuth, Thomas Hart Benton, Jo Davidson, Yasuo Kuniyoshi, William Zorach, Hugo Robus, and Isamu Noguchi. The Whitney Museum of American Art opened on November 18, 1931, featuring Gertrude Vanderbilt Whitney's collection of over 500 artworks, including paintings, sculpture, and graphic arts created after 1900, figurative artists of the 1920s, and the Social Realists. The Whitney has since added Hard-Edge Abstractionists, Magic Realists, Abstract Expressionists, Color Field artists, New Naturalists, New Realists, Pop artists, Conceptualists, and all the other schools. The broad scope of these collections has put the Whitney in the front ranks of American museums.

The perfectly preserved row of buildings on the south side of East 8th Street, numbers 6–26, were built in 1834 and 1835 and were remodeled in 1916 for conversion into apartments by the owner, Sailors' Snug Harbor; Maynicke & Franke were the architects. This picturesque group of buildings is of a type unique to Greenwich Village. Their light-colored, smooth-stuccoed facades represent a Germanic version of Mediterranean styles, giving the group a basically symmetrical appearance. Throughout this row of houses, most of the arches and many of the square-headed lintels are made of natural-colored brick that contrasts with the bare stucco walls, giving these features extra emphasis.

The legendary **Cedar Street Tavern** lives on, in name only, at 82 University Place (at 10th Street). The original barroom (on University Place off 8th Street) was frequented in the early 1950s by artists Jackson Pollock, Willem de Kooning, Franz Kline, Mark Rothko, John Chamberlain, Philip Guston, Larry Rivers, Audrey Flack, and Ruth Kligman. When the bar suffered severe fire damage, it moved up the street, and over the years has become a quiet, conservative local pub, complete with wood paneling, exposed brick walls, hanging ferns, and Tiffany-style ceiling lamps. It is a popular lunchtime hangout, and was designed by architect Tony Vercesi.

The Cedar Street Tavern on closing night, March 30, 1963

The original Cedar Street Tavern at 24 University Place (at 8th Street) had the distinction of not being on Cedar Street; it had no TV, no jukebox or Muzak, no skeetball. But it was *the* New York School artists' bar. Made famous by those internationally renowned art-world stars, it became the favorite watering place for painters and sculptors, actors and directors, writers, poets, and editors who lived in or visited New York. There were Beat authors Allen Ginsberg, Jack Kerouac, Gregory Corso, Jack Micheline, and Ted Joans; poets Diane diPrima and Joel Oppenheimer; author/activist LeRoi Jones; print curator Paul Cummings; radical poet and publisher Tuli Kupferberg; art critic and poet Frank O'Hara; writers Hubert Selby and Paul Goodman; Living Theatre founders Julian Beck and Judith Malina; and composer and musician David Amram.

There was no attempt to brighten up the decor of the old bar—it was almost depressing in its starkness: the long bar in front, leading

37

back to a harshly lit space with bare walls, wooden booths lined with metal studs, and small tables. The food was strictly "pub grub," with meat loaf and mashed potatoes a weekly special. Raucous tales of drunken brawls that took place at the Cedar usually starred Pollock, whose antics caused many of them. His wife, Lee Krasner, never accompanied him to the bar. Sadly, his alcoholism finally led to his death in a fatal auto accident in East Hampton. In their Pulitzer Prize-winning autobiography of Pollock, Steven Naifeh and Gregory White Smith accurately portray the role of the Cedar Street Tavern in Pollock's saga: "For Jackson it was a weekly trip back in time, back to the rim of the Grand Canyon to entertain the road crew with his drunken stumblings."

For younger artists and lesser stars as well, the Cedar served as a meeting place, a club, a place where they could catch up on the latest art-world gossip, and find a sympathetic ear to talk about their own work.

A rundown town house at 27 West 8th Street (at the foot of MacDougal Street) has an honored place in literary history as the site where Margaret Anderson published *The Little Review.* The magazine was started in 1914 in Chicago, where Anderson, inspired by the politically oriented *New Masses,* dreamed of publishing a journal dedicated to the most avant-garde literature of the day. Her determination and the force of her personality became legendary as she recruited numerous first-rank talents, including writers Jean Cocteau, Ezra Pound, T. S. Eliot, and Edgar Lee Masters. When Greenwich Village became the center of American literary life in the teens, it seemed natural for Anderson to move her magazine to the heart of Bohemia. In a daring move, particularly since she had no financing, Anderson and her assistant editor, jane heap (who always signed her name in lower-case letters) relocated to the heart of Greenwich Village and resumed publication of the *The Little Review.*

After a few moves, the editorial offices settled at 27 West 8th Street, in the same building with The Washington Square Book Shop, already one of its supporters. On the second floor, Egmont Arens, co-owner of the bookstore, was publishing a handsome, large-format art, photography, and poetry magazine called *Playboy.* Anderson and heap also lived in the building in what can best be described as eccentric surroundings. Their friends and contributors were equally extraordinary. There was, for example, the Baroness Elsa von Freytag von Loringhoven, whose poetry Anderson called "perhaps the best of any woman's of our time." Once the Baroness shaved her head and painted her bare skull bright red, then rushed over to the 8th Street apartment and announced, "Shaving one's head is like having a new love experience." To cap her performance, she shed her clothes, saying, "It's better when I'm nude."

Thanks to the efforts of the magazine's self-appointed foreign editor, Ezra Pound, it achieved its greatest fame and immortality in literary history. It was Pound who sent in a manuscript by the then little-known writer James Joyce. Anderson recognized its worth, and began publishing installments from Joyce's novel *Ulysses* in the magazine. In response to a complaint from the Society for the Suppression of Vice, *The Little Review* was indicted for publishing Joyce's episode describing Leopold Bloom's erotic thoughts. The magazine was found guilty and fined $100. But Anderson and heap were not deterred, subsequent issues had more installments of *Ulysses,* although eventually the plan to publish the entire novel was abandoned. The magazine suffered from continuing money problems. A promised $4,000 contribution from Otto Hermann Kahn, a banker and chairman of the board of the Metropolitan Opera, failed to materialize. Anderson and heap, apparently discouraged, transferred their publication to Paris.

Sixth Avenue is the dividing line between the Washington Square area and the West Village. The open space at the Village Square, where there is now a community garden, resulted from the removal of the old Sixth Avenue elevated train tracks in 1938 and also the dreaded Women's House of Detention.

Sixth Avenue (aka Avenue of the Americas) is not exactly steeped in history but is probably most notable for the notorious and shabby Irish saloons that thrived there during prohibition. The Golden Swan, fondly called The Hell Hole or Bucket of Blood, was at Sixth Avenue and 4th Street; the site is now an empty lot. It had sawdust on the floor, beat-up wooden tables, and reeked of stale beer. Tom Wallace, an ex-prizefighter and its owner, kept a pig in the cellar, feeding it garbage scraps that were left by the free-lunch crowd.

The saloon was patronized by gamblers, pimps, prostitutes, anarchists, politicians, longshoremen, and the feared Hudson Dusters gang. It also became a haunt of writers and artists intrigued by the criminal element who hung out there. Eugene O'Neill found inspira-

Jefferson Market Library

tion for his plays at The Hell Hole (including *The Iceman Cometh*), Dorothy Day, founder of the *Catholic Worker,* material for her journalism, and both Charles Demuth and John Sloan recorded their impressions of it on canvas. Malcolm Cowley described the unique relation between the dark underside of New York society and the literati who frequented the bar in his book *Exile's Return:* "The gangsters admired Dorothy Day because she could drink them under the table, but they felt more at home with Eugene O'Neill, who listened to their troubles and never criticized." During prohibition, the influence of its proprietor with Tammany Hall insured that alcohol flowed freely within.

From a small neighborhood produce market at the Village Square, **Balducci's**, at 424 Sixth Avenue (at 9th Street), has evolved into a gastronomic supermarket crammed full of gourmet treats, as well as a tourist attraction. Top-quality produce is the centerpiece of this family-owned store, and beautifully arranged displays of fresh fruits and vegetables all seem to glow at the peak of perfection.

Enticing trays of ready-to-eat salads, fish and meat entrees, and Italian specialties are featured at a horseshoe-shaped counter in the center of the store. The cheese counter has an indepth selection of over 300 varieties, and after making their selection, customers can head over to the bakery section to find fresh-baked breads of every conceivable variety, including muffins, croissants, brioches, and bagels. The cake-and-candy department features seasonal and dramatically composed treats ranging from tiny fruit tarts to pumpkin pie and towering confections of chocolate, hazelnut, and mocha creams. The seafood counter offers both exotic and everyday species—from fresh-caught trout to New Zealand scallops; the meat department carries game, free-range poultry, and a full selection of beef, veal, and lamb cuts. A deluxe foodstore with an authentic, and noisy, Italian ambience, Balducci's has been a Village tradition since it opened in 1945.

The **Jefferson Market Court House** at Sixth Avenue and 10th Street is a fine specimen of civic Victoriana. This neo-Gothic extrava-ganza has tracery windows, numerous gargoyles, pyramid, mansard, and gabled roofs, red-and-black brick designs adorning the facade, and an imposing clock tower that overlooks its low-rise neighbors. Built in 1876 according to plans by architects Frederick Clark Withers and Calvert Vaux, this Village landmark stands on grounds once occupied by a courthouse complex that also included a jail, which was

The Spanish-Portuguese Cemetery of Shearith Israel

later replaced with the Women's House of Detention (since demolished). Used as a courthouse until 1945, the building later accommodated various civic agencies.

By the early '60s, the courthouse stood empty and faced imminent destruction. Village residents, led by preservation activist Ruth Wittenberg, fought successfully to keep the building intact. Accurately restored from old plans by architect Giorgio Cavaglieri, the courthouse reopened in 1967 as a local branch library and community center. It is a Village monument, not only to the exuberance of Victorian architecture, but also to the inspiring achievement of an aroused citizenry.

The **Spanish-Portuguese Cemetery of Shearith Israel**, sandwiched between 72 and 76 West 11th Street, was opened in 1805 and closed in 1829 when 11th Street was routed through the land. It is one of the oldest and smallest cemeteries in the city. The Sephardic congregation represented the earliest Jewish settlers in New York, dating from 1654, when a group of Spanish and Portuguese Jews landed in New Amsterdam. The cemetery on 11th Street was their second burial ground; the remains of the first can be seen in Chinatown at Chatham Square. A third cemetery was laid out in Chelsea on 21st Street, between Sixth and Seventh Avenues, after this plot was reduced to its present-day tiny triangular shape when 11th Street was constructed. A low masonry wall surmounted by an iron fence encloses the cemetery. A gate at the center gives access to this little graveyard, which still has some of its original tombstones, including a stone obelisk.

Patchin Place, just off 10th Street, near Sixth Avenue, is a tiny secluded nondescript dead-end courtyard perhaps less then 200 feet long that faces the north side of the Jefferson Market library. It is protected by an iron gate and most people pass by without ever

Patchin Place

noticing the hidden street. All the houses on Patchin Place were built by Aaron D. Patchin in 1848 in the vernacular style of the period. It is believed that all the buildings were built as boardinghouses for Basque waiters who worked at the old Brevoort Hotel. But this is unlikely because the Brevoort had not yet been built.

This courtyard has been the home of many important literary figures. Harry Kemp, the hatless poet, and Gaston Lachaise, the sculptor, lived here. The poet e. e. cummings lived at number 4 Patchin Place from 1923 until his death in 1962. John Reed, the radical author, moved with Louise Bryant to Patchin Place in the years just before he died in 1920.

Its most illustrious tenant was Djuna Barnes, who first encountered the Bohemian Village in the early teens as a cub reporter for the *Brooklyn Eagle.* She lived at 5 Patchin Place. Her articles about the neighborhood's Left Bank idiosyncrasies, accompanied by her witty illustrations, enjoyed great popularity. An eccentric in her own right, Barnes felt at home in the Village, falling in league with the radical clique of writers and artists who patronized Bruno's Garret. The black-caped, chain-smoking figure became a familiar sight at the Café Lafayette, where she often retreated to write. Until her departure for Paris at the end of the First World War, Barnes found the Village a stimulating tonic for her literary experiments. *The Book of Repulsive Women*, a controversial collection of verse, and three scripts for the Provincetown Players (of which she was a founding member), were among the writings she produced in this period.

As the clouds of war gathered in the '30s, some of the expatriates began returning home, including Barnes who came back to 5 Patchin Place. The publication of her extraordinary novel, *Nightwood*, in Paris in 1936 had made her reputation. It was about a psychopathic woman who destroys those nearest her—her husband, her son, two women who love her—and is told Greek-chorus style by a physician. T. S. Eliot, who wrote an introduction for the book, admired "the great achievement of a style, the beauty of phrasing, the brilliance of wit and characterization, and a quality of horror and doom very nearly related to that of Elizabethan tragedy." Eliot said it was "so good a novel that only sensibilities trained in poetry can wholly appreciate it." Back in New York, Djuna Barnes lived the life of a recluse and died in 1982 at the age of 90.

Flavor-Cup coffee is the house brand at **Schapira Coffee Company**, 117 West 10th Street (at Greenwich Avenue), a little shop that sells aromatic coffees and teas, and attractive kitchenware for brewing these essential beverages. The virgin beans are roasted right on the premises by Master Roaster Ron Bowen, which accounts for the really rich flavor of the coffee. Light enters the warm interior of this neighborhood favorite via a Colonial-style bow window, and the decor is equally atmospheric, with burlap bags of coffee beans taking up much of the floor space. American, Italian, and French roasts, with all kinds of variations and permutations of coffee bean, are ground to order. The tea offerings include old favorites as well as exotic blends. Also on hand for gift buyers are pretty decorated tins to hold the fragrant coffees or teas.

Directly around the corner from Patchin Place, on the west side of Sixth Avenue, is **Milligan Place**. It has four houses built in 1852, and closely resembles Patchin Place. Like its neighbor, it was constructed by Aaron D. Patchin, whose father-in-law, Samuel Milligan, owned the land. The narrow entrance is through a cast-iron gate with an archway that spells out Milligan Place. This little courtyard is particularly fortunate because its small entranceway from Sixth Avenue effectively cuts it off from the noise of that busy thoroughfare.

Because Milligan owned land inside this block, it probably served his property, and thus it was given his name.

The north side of Milligan Place faces the side wall of No. 453 Sixth Avenue. George Cram Cook (founder, director, and guiding spirit of the Provincetown Players) and his wife Susan Glaspell (playwright and novelist) lived on Milligan Place from 1913 to 1917.

The New School for Social Research at 66 West 12th Street was founded in 1919 and is a pioneer in the field of adult education. Its founders included such outstanding scholars as historians Charles Beard and James Harvey

Djuna Barnes shopping on Greenwich Avenue, August 14, 1959

Robinson and economist Alvin Johnson, who was the school's president for over twenty years. Early faculty members were the economist Thorstein Veblen and John Dewey, father of progressive education in America. When the Nazis began their conquest of Europe, the New School formed its noted "University in Exile" by inviting refugee scholars to join its faculty.

The striking architecture of the original building is best seen from across the street. As the eye traverses the facade, the whole front of the structure seems to slant backward because the banks of windows are spaced progressively closer together as they ascend. This architectural device serves to strengthen the illusion of height and makes the building seem smaller than it is. The building was designed by Joseph Urban and constructed in 1931.

A mural by José Clemente Orozco on the fifth floor depicts international attempts to achieve brotherhood. The fresco includes portraits of Lenin, leader of the Russian Revolution; Felipe Carillo Puerto, a Mexican hero of independence; and India's great leader Mohandas Gandhi. A series of murals by Thomas Hart Benton was on the third floor for over fifty years, until it was stripped off the wall and sold to the Equitable Insurance Company, which now displays the restored artwork in the lobby of their skyscraper on Seventh Avenue and 51st Street. A sculpture court and garden link the West 12th Street building with a modern annex facing West 11th Street.

The Dial's offices were in a brownstone at 152 West 13th Street, now a private school. The magazine was founded in 1840 in Cambridge, Massachusetts as an organ for the transcendentalists, with Margaret Fuller, and later Ralph Waldo Emerson, as editor. It was discontinued, then revived, and over the years went through numerous changes to emerge again in 1917 in New York with a "socially analytical and humanitarian emphasis." In 1920, The Dial was sold to Scofield Thayer and J. Sibley Watson, Jr. who made it a nonpolitical monthly of arts and letters. It quickly became the best of all the avant-garde publications, featuring distinguished writers and artists from both Europe and America. In a typical issue dated December 1920, Joseph Conrad contributed prefaces from three of his novels; Osbert Sitwell published a poem; there is a long letter from Ezra Pound; Alice Corbin is represented by two short poems; T. S. Eliot has an article on Matthew Arnold; and Shane Leslie (editor of The Dublin Review) reviewed a 1,240-page book, The First World War. The masthead lists Scofield Thayer as editor and Gilbert Seldes as associate editor. Seldes became a Village Voice critic in 1955. When Marianne Moore first submitted her poems to The Dial, they were rejected. But in 1924, she received the Dial Award, and in 1925, she became editor of the magazine until it closed in 1929.

The **Lesbian and Gay Community** Services Center, 208 West 13th Street (at Seventh Avenue), occupies an 1842 red-brick former school building, originally P.S. 6, then the Food and Maritime Trades High School. After the high school closed, the building stood vacant until the Center, a nonprofit corporation, bought the building from the city in 1984 to provide space for organizations delivering social, medical, and cultural services to the lesbian and gay communities. Over 250 groups rent space at the Center for meetings and other events. Six organizations are headquartered there: The Coalition for Lesbian and Gay Rights, Community Health Project, Lesbian Switchboard, Metropolitan Community Church of New York, NYC Gay and Lesbian Anti-Violence Project, and SAGE (Senior Action in a Gay Environment). A library, family center, shows, readings, and New York City orientation are some of the programs operated at the Center. The National Museum of Lesbian and Gay History and Archive was launched there in 1989 and will be the first museum in the U.S. devoted to lesbian and gay concerns. The Museum Committee produces exhibitions and the Archive provides resources for researchers.

Directly across the street from the Lesbian and Gay Community Services Center, at 215 West 13th Street, is the building where Anaïs Nin lived in the 1930s. She paid $60 a month rent for a skylight studio on the top floor. She eventually started her own press at 17 East 13th Street. Nin was among the legendary Village literary figures, much of her fame due to her torrid romance with Henry Miller, which was portrayed in the 1990 movie *Henry and June*, and her extremely popular *Diary*.

Anaïs Nin was born in Paris to parents of mixed Spanish-Cuban descent. She worked as a dancer, teacher, lecturer, novelist, literary critic, and diarist. She studied psychoanalysis in Paris under Otto Rank. In 1932 she published a critical work, *D. H. Lawrence: An Unprofessional Study*. Her first novel, *House of Incest*, a treatment of narcissism, was published in 1936. Of her later books, she said: "I write as a poet in the framework of prose and appear to claim the rights of a novelist. . . . I intend the greater part of my writing to be received directly through the senses, as one apprehends painting and music."

Her fiction also includes *Winter of Artifice* (1939), a psychiatric investigation of a father's and a daughter's relationship; *Under a Glass Bell* (1944), a collection of stories; *This Hunger* (1945), interrelated stories about women who fear human society in general, and men in particular; *Ladders to Fire* (1946), stories of women who search for their identity; *The Four-Chambered Heart* (1950), a novel about a triangular love conflict; and *A Spy in the House of Love* (1954), on a woman's self-questioning about her many transient love affairs.

After her death, her editor, Gunther Stuhlmann, brought out *The Diary of Anaïs Nin* in five volumes. Her reputation as an artist and seminal figure in the new Feminism of the 1970s rests on these journals written from 1931 to 1974, which are an engrossing record of an era and some of its most intriguing and avant-garde personalities, as well as "a passionate, explicit, and candid account of one woman's voyage of self-discovery."

The radical magazine called *The Masses* descended from a muckraking Socialist publication founded in 1911 by a Dutch immigrant

Anaïs Nin with Ted Wilentz, owner of the 8th Street Bookshop, at a Living Theatre performance, December 20, 1960

named Piet Vlag. Although the magazine folded in less than a year, its contributors banded together to revive it. The group, headed by cartoonist Art Young, invited Max Eastman to serve as editor without pay; he was later joined by Floyd Dell as managing editor. Maintaining the name, left-wing politics, and principles of collective ownership of its model, the new *Masses* set up editorial offices in a former plumbing supply store at 91 Greenwich Avenue, now a video store in a new apartment house.

John Reed, who would be buried within the walls of the Kremlin, wrote the statement of purpose for the publication: "To everlastingly attack old systems, old morals, old prejudices. . . ." *The Masses* took up the causes of Feminism, black civil rights, sexual freedom, birth control, and Pacifism. Work was donated by such talents as illustrator Jo Davidson and writers Walter Lippmann, Wilbur Daniel Steele, Carl Sandburg, Sherwood Anderson, Louis Untermeyer, and Amy Lowell.

The art that enlivened *The Masses* encompassed many styles, from realism to sharp satire. The cartoons were memorably caustic—

48

especially those depicting bloated, top-hatted capitalists stepping on the backs of the proletariat. Even after America entered World War I, *The Masses* championed Pacifism and Socialism, calling on President Wilson to repeal the draft. The editors were twice indicted and brought to trial; although no convictions resulted, the magazine was banned from newsstands. After the Post Office revoked its second-class mailing privileges, *The Masses* could no longer afford to publish; it closed in December 1917.

Reds, a fascinating movie directed by Warren Beatty in 1981, recounted the history of many personalities associated with *The Masses.* Perhaps the most romantic of these left-wing radicals was John Reed. Raised on the West Coast in bourgeois comfort, he attended Harvard College, spent a brief time in Paris, and then headed for Greenwich Village, where he quickly acquired celebrity as a playboy and propagandist, involved in most of the political controversies of his day. An enthusiastic supporter of *The Masses,* he wrote his first article for the magazine on the 1913 Paterson silk workers' strike.

Along with other Village personalities, he frequented Mabel Dodge's salon on lower Fifth Avenue, and the two became lovers. But the strongest influence on his life would come not from a love affair, but from a country. Sent as a foreign correspondent to Europe by *Metropolitan* magazine, he was totally infatuated with the Russian people. On his return from Russia, Reed met Louise Bryant, who lived with him on and off for the rest of his life.

Reed's best-known work was the classic celebration of the 1917 Russian Revolution, *Ten Days that Shook the World,* written in his room over Polly's Restaurant. Convinced of the virtues of the revolution and persecuted by political red-hunting in the U.S., Reed eventually returned to Russia to live. He was only thirty-three when he died in Moscow of typhus.

In a class by itself is the legendary **Village Vanguard,** 178 Seventh Avenue South (near West 11th Street). The roster of artists who have performed here over six decades reads like a *Who's Who* of jazz history. Still one of the best places to hear contemporary jazz, the club is in a basement space once occupied by a speakeasy. Max Gordon, who opened the club on his arrival in New York in 1936, originally hailed from Portland, Oregon. His parents wanted him to attend law school, but his ambition was to go to Greenwich Village and do something creative. And that is exactly what he did.

Gordon booked such jazz greats as saxophonists John Coltrane, Dexter Gordon, and Sonny Rollins; bebop greats Theolonius Monk, Charlie Parker, and Dizzy Gillespie; brothers Thad, Hank, and Elton Jones; folk legends like Leadbelly; contemporary jazz stars like Keith Jarrett; bandleaders Woody Shaw and Art Blakey—the list is endless. But the Vanguard has been a showcase for more than music. Gordon also booked singers, poets, comics, and mimes, and, in some cases, made the careers of such stars as singers Pearl Bailey and Sarah Vaughan; comedians Mike Nichols and Elaine May, Jerry Stiller and Anne Meara, Mort Sahl, Wally Cox, and Woody Allen; Beat writer Jack Kerouac; and folk stars Burl Ives and The Kingston Trio.

More good music is provided at the bustling music club **Chicago B.L.U.E.S.**, 73 Eighth Avenue (at 13th Street). This branch-office of the famous Midwestern club features "only Chicago-area blues artists working with their regular Chicago blues bands." For those who want their blues unadulterated, this is the place to go.

If there ever was a real working class bar, the **Eagle Tavern**, 355 West 14th Street (at Hudson Street), certainly fits the description. On the northern fringes of the Village, near the Gansevoort meat market, this nearly 100-year-old bar features an assortment of Celtic, English, and American folk musicians. One can listen, as I did living over the bar in the early 1950s, sing along, or dance to Irish and other Celtic music, alternating with bluegrass and other ethnic and regional folk music Wednesday nights and weekends. An open Irish music session is offered on Monday evenings, so bring your bodhran!

Bleecker Street/West 4th Street

The Village Gate; The Bottom Line; Collector's Stadium; Village Chess Shop; The Bitter End; Circle-in-the-Square; *The Fantastiks*/Sullivan Street Playhouse; Fiorello H. La Guardia; Bleecker Street; Street fairs; Cafés; Specialty Stores; Greenwich House; Ridiculous Theatrical Company; West 4th Street

The Village Gate, 160 Bleecker Street (at Thompson Street), is a must stop for both tourists and performers passing through town. Jazz greats, comedic talents, cabaret shows, and off-Broadway hits have all graced Art D'Lugoff's basement stage. Aretha Franklin had her first Big Apple stage date here. D'Lugoff booked jazz legends Dizzy Gillespie, Miles Davis, Charles Mingus, Theolonius Monk, and folk-singer Harry Belafonte, to name a few. The Gate has put on shows that not only have run the gamut of tastes and styles, but also have been at the forefront of American theatre. Some examples are *Jacques Brel Is Alive and Well and Living in Paris, Macbird* (a satire of Lyndon B. Johnson and the Vietnam War), and a dramatization of *The Brady Bunch* episodes. D'Lugoff has also generously offered his space for scores of benefits over the years, for causes ranging from striking newspaper workers to AIDS research. The building that houses The Gate is also of note. The 1892 Mills House was built as a men's dormitory and shelter when Bleecker Street was a seedy, dangerous

The Bottom Line

strip. The building is now a luxury condo; the main stage for The Gate is in what used to be the laundry room for the hotel.

Folk music gets most of the publicity, but rock and roll thrives in Greenwich Village. Probably the top area room is **The Bottom Line**, 15 West 4th Street. Even before Bruce Springsteen gave his now legendary 1975 set, The Bottom Line has been the biggest of the small clubs. Rolling Stone Keith Richards turns up on stage sometimes, New York bands like The Ramones or Lou Reed played there early on, and out-of-town performers like Joe Jackson, Elvis Costello, and R.E.M. know they've made it when they play here. Nearby, on Bleecker Street between La Guardia Place and MacDougal Street, less famous—but plenty rocking—bands play Kenny's Castaways and The Back Fence.

The **Collector's Stadium**, 214 Sullivan Street (at West 4th Street), is a home run on any fan's scorecard. In the old days, a store featuring baseball cards and related memorabilia would be filled with knee-high fourth graders waving coins at the counter. Now, of course, sports collecting is a big business, and most of the children in stores like this are watching their parents write out a check for a 1951 rookie

Mickey Mantle card, an old bleacher seat from Ebbets Field, or a pair of Dorothy Hamill ice skates.

Collector's Stadium is one of the city's largest, best-stocked, and most entertaining memorabilia stores. The walls are covered with old football, basketball, hockey, and baseball uniforms, team yearbooks and media guides, baseball gloves, hockey sticks, autographed balls, audio and video cassettes of big games, and various old promotional items like caps, bags, and dolls.

Oh yes—there are also baseball cards. Everything from 19th-century cigarette cards, to the

The Village Chess Shop

newer models from Donruss, Fleer Upper Deck, and the granddaddy of them all, the Brooklyn-based Topps, are here in mass quantities. Even if you don't want to lay out $1,200 for a 1967 Tom Seaver, the Collector's Stadium is a veritable sports museum for young and old.

For chess fans, there are the free, outdoor, concrete chess-and-checkers tables in the southwest corner of Washington Square Park. But for those desiring indoor games, a cup of coffee to help you mull over your next move, and facilities including regulation timers, boards, and players of all levels, the **Village Chess Shop**, 230 Thompson Street, is the place to go. It is a warm, friendly, intimate room with the best chess in town. Plus, if you're in the mood for a game against a computer, you'll find one here. They also have all kinds of chessboards and pieces—in alabaster, onyx, or Egyptian camel bone—for sale. The store opened in the wake of Bobby Fischer winning the world chess championship and has been busy ever since.

At 147 Bleecker Street (corner La Guardia Place) is **The Bitter End**, a legendary Village folk-music and comedy club. At one time, you could hear everyone from Woody Allen to Peter, Paul, and Mary here, or pick up a guitar and join in on "Hootenanny night." On March 13, 1963 boxing's heavyweight champion Muhammad Ali (aka Cassius Clay) read poetry here. Like many other clubs, The Bitter End now features new wave and progressive rock groups, catering to the student population in the neighborhood.

The **Circle-in-the-Square**, 159 Bleecker Street (at Thompson Street), occupies the site of the former Amato Opera company. Although the theatre's name is hallowed in dramatic history, this performance space is actually now let out to varying groups and has no connection with the original company, which was a significant force in the development of off-Broadway theatre. The original company started in the early '50s on Sheridan Square (in the old Greenwich Village Inn) as "The Loft Players." Ted Mann and José Quintero had formed the company in Woodstock in the summer of 1949. They decided to move to New York, and discovered the abandoned Greenwich Village Inn with a "For Rent" sign on it one night while taking a walk after dinner. The unusual space—dominated by several large pillars—led them to develop a theatre-in-the-round, from which the name "Circle" in the "Square" comes. Its famous productions included Federico Garcia Lorca's *Yerma* and *If Five Years Pass,* Alberto Moravia's *The Girl on the Via Flaminia,* Truman Capote's *The Grass Harp,* Christopher Fry's *The Lady's Not for Burning,* and the famous Eugene O'Neill drama *The Iceman Cometh.*

The Circle-in-the-Square established a series of Sunday-afternoon programs called *The Theatre Circle* directed by the Greek scholar Kimon Friar. His programs in the early '50s included poetry readings, concerts, and lectures by such outstanding playwrights as William Inge, Truman Capote, Arthur Miller, Tennessee Williams, and Lillian Hellman, and writers Gore Vidal, Vinnette Carroll, Theodore Roethke, and Dorothy Parker. The famous theatre can claim among its alumni Geraldine Page, who played in *Summer and Smoke;* and Jason Robards, Jr., whose career was launched by his portrayal of Hickey in the 1956 production of O'Neill's *Iceman.* José Quintero achieved widespread acclaim for his directorial talent shown off at the theatre.

In 1959, the Greenwich Village Inn was torn down and replaced by an apartment building. The company moved to its new home on Bleecker Street in a space that had been a standard, proscenium theatre. Quintero adapted it to be a three-quarter round stage. Jean Genet's *The Balcony* and Thornton Wilder's *Plays for Bleecker Street* were among the successes at the Bleecker Street location.

54

The American musical theatre's longest running production, *The Fantastiks*, now in its fourth decade, is advancing toward its 15,000th performance. *The Fantastiks*, the creation of Tom Jones (book and lyrics) and Harvey Schmidt (music) is still performed at the **Sullivan Street Playhouse** where it opened on May 3, 1960. The show was backed with an original investment of only $16,500; in the '90s it might have cost $165,000 to produce. There have been more than 11,000 productions of *The Fantastiks* in the world, including professional, stock, amateur, community, college, and even high-school productions; the show has established a record in Tokyo, running for twenty years, and it has played in Budapest, Beijing, Bangkok, Bombay, and many other cities around the world. It was one of the first musicals to receive an OBIE from the *Village Voice*. *The Fantastiks*'s run is surpassed only by *The Mousetrap*, Agatha Christie's mystery play, which opened in London in 1952. It has survived newspaper strikes, blizzards, actors' strikes, electrical blackouts, and a building collapse on the block.

The Sullivan Street Playhouse was a blacksmith shop and a stable for horses. In the 1920s it was a famous nightclub named Jimmy Kelly's, a speakeasy frequented by celebrities, politicians, and members of the underworld. The basement walk-in refrigerator used by Kelly's is now a walk-in closet used to store extra costumes. The famous Village club featured fan dancers and "14 lovely ladies mostly unadorned," as described in an old guide.

Fiorello H. La Guardia, perhaps the most famous native son of Greenwich Village, was born in a row house, now demolished, next to the Playhouse. The first Italian-American to be elected to Congress, he was mayor of New York from 1934 to 1945. A memorial statue of La Guardia is planned for the park strip on La Guardia Place north of Bleecker.

Although **Bleecker Street** between Sixth and Seventh Avenues is no longer lined with old-time Italian street peddlers hawking fruits and vegetables from their pushcarts, a surprisingly strong Old-World Italian flavor—and great specialty foodstores—still pervades this northern outpost of Little Italy. The continuing presence of Our Lady of Pompeii Roman Catholic Church and School, at the corner of Bleecker and Father Demo Square, is one reason for the ethnic stability of the neighborhood. The church's annual festival is a great occasion, replacing the flow of Bleecker Street traffic with booths that

Chuck Mangione (l) and Maynard Ferguson (r) at the Blue Note, May 24, 1988

spread for two blocks up Carmine Street from the corner of Bleecker, offering games of chance, Italian and other ethnic food specialties, and children's rides and games.

Another colorful street fair is held nearby in late May-early June from Houston to Spring Streets, sponsored by St. Anthony's Church and School. At night Sullivan and MacDougal Streets are bedecked with arches of lights, and crowds surge up and down the traffic-free streets, in search of the perfect sausage sandwich and deliciously deep-fried zeppole (balls of dough that are fried, then sprinkled with powdered sugar), followed by an inevitable attack of heartburn. Sodas, beers, Italian ices, candy, nuts, and pizzas are all on tap, along with all the games of a carnival midway, including a Ferris wheel. A street procession with a relic of St. Anthony is the highlight of the event. New York's other great Italian street fair is the Feast of San Gennaro, held in the fall, on Mulberry Street, north of Canal Street.

Caffè Lucca, 228 Bleecker Street (at Sixth Avenue), has four outdoor tables facing Father Demo Square and intimate round marble-topped tables inside. Serving cappuccino, pastry, espresso, hot chocolate, and light bites, it's a typically European-style café, with a strong Italian accent.

It's hard to believe that the unpretentious luncheonette at the corner of Carmine Street gets rave reviews from restaurant critics, but Italian Home Cooking, 232 Bleecker Street, regardless of its barebones decor, deserves the kudos. Six stools at a Formica counter, red-and-white checked cloths on the tables, and a red-and-white tile floor are all the ambience you'll get here. But after enjoying a bowl of the homemade minestrone soup or other homemade daily specials and noting the inexpensive prices, customers do not complain.

Collectors will recognize the appeal—and bargain prices—at the Golden Disc, 239 Bleecker Street (at Cornelia Street). Nostalgic browsers can pore over such items as *Billboard* magazine's top rock-and-roll hits of the 1950s, Pat Boone song sheets, or an album cover of the Cadets greatest hits. The record bins have miles and miles of soul, reggae, folk, doowop, a cappella, and even long-forgotten waltz music. The walls are completely covered with 45-rpm covers.

Rocco's Pastry Shop and Café, 243 Bleecker, and Lucia Bleecker Street Pastry, 245 Bleecker, lure passersby with windows filled with fresh-baked goodies. Inside, each bakery shop has a distinctive café with espresso machine at the ready, and tempting display cases. In Rocco's, the gray marble-topped tables can accommodate customers with a choice of coffees and miniature Italian cannoli, a baba au rhum, or a nut-, chocolate chip-, fruit-, or whipped-cream-topped pastry. Next door in Lucia's, intimate, round pink-marble-topped tables are featured, the espresso machine is against the back wall, and color photos of Italy make a nice backdrop for wafting in an eclair, a Napoléon, or a custard-filled fruit tart. The selections are awesome, the atmosphere casual, the experience mouthwatering.

The Cornelia Street Café, 29 Cornelia Street (at Bleecker Street), is a unique café, restaurant, and cabaret, a Village culinary and cultural landmark since 1977. Its whitewashed brick walls, arched doorways, and original art make for a classic Bohemian look, enhanced, in fine weather, by sidewalk tables at the French doors. Open from breakfast till late night, the café offers all three meals, plus light bites throughout the day. The food is fresh, with specialties like home-baked muffins, soufflé-like quiches, and delicious almond bread pudding. Founded by three artists, the café still has a special regard for the performing arts. Prose and poetry readings, jazz, folk, and pop music, cabaret, and theatre productions make for a full calendar of events almost nightly. There's nourishment for the soul as well as the stomach in this simpatico place.

Off-Off Broadway, as the *Village Voice* christened it, became a whole new category of theatrical entertainment that offered a cabaret-style showcase for young dramatic talent. The idea of a café-theatre for short plays was first conceived in the middle 1950s by Rick Allman of the Café Bizarre. It wasn't until 1958 that Joe Cino's Caffè Cino gave the movement added momentum. Cino opened his coffeehouse in a narrow storefront at 133 Cornelia Street. The atmosphere was friendly and nonpressured, intimate and warm. At first the café put on poetry readings. This was in the heyday of the Beat era and readings in many Village coffeehouses showcased the work of Beat poets. At Caffè Cino from time to time there were also readings of excerpts from plays, and these evolved into performances of short plays. Cino encouraged young playwrights, among them such luminaries-to-be as Lanford Wilson and Tom Eyen. Money troubles plagued Cino, and the café also suffered severe fire damage in April 1965. It closed in 1968, one year after Cino's death by his own hand. Today the Cornelia Street Café, which has theatrical and musical performances along with its café-restaurant offerings, seems to be carrying on the artistic spirit of the old Caffè Cino.

Murray's Cheese Shop, 257 Bleecker Street (at Cornelia Street), is a Village institution. Formerly located right across the street, Murray's consistently offers unbeatable prices for cheeses of all nations. Whether it's French Brie or Camembert, Italian Gorgonzola, English Cotswold, Austrian Swiss, American cheddar, or Danish blue, it is for sale in the aromatic confines of this small shop. At the back of the store are vats of olives and feta cheese, and smoked meats are strung from the ceiling. Fancy mustards and fresh breads are here too.

A. Zito & Son, 259 Bleecker Street, sells nothing but bread—fresh daily, baked in the basement ovens, white or whole wheat, with sesame seeds or without, with a few Italian specialty breads available from time to time. The store was immortalized in a classic 1930s photo by Berenice Abbott of the front window, and the storefront today remains unchanged. A no-frills classic.

Faicco's, 260 Bleecker Street, specializes in meat products such as homemade sausages seasoned with herbs and spices (made on the premises), smoked meats and sala-mis, and ready-to-cook beef and chicken entrees. A well-rounded antipasto platter could be created from its pickled mushrooms, olive trays, and prepared salads. Bril-liant white tiles make a sharp back-drop for displays of imported olive oils, vinegars, tomatoes, pastas,

Faicco's

58

fresh breads, dried mushrooms, and cheeses. Gourmet Italian-style items at their best.

Aphrodisia, 264 Bleecker Street, brings a gentle New Age atmosphere to the street, with herbs and essential oils that offer spice for food, remedies for relaxation or mental or physical well-being, or maybe just to perfume the bath for a touch of pampered luxury. There are some appealing gift items—colored bath salts, artfully boxed potpourris, scented soaps, and lotions—as well as a full line of cooking herbs and teas, plus dried fruits, candy, and an esoteric collection of nutrition books. Just browsing here is enough to expand your consciousness.

Whether you're searching for that elusive vintage prewar Martin D-45 or your taste runs more toward Fender Stratocasters, you shouldn't miss the nationally renowned Matt Umanov Guitar store at 273 Bleecker Street. Here guitar aficionados hungrily eye some of the most beautiful and rare acoustic and electric guitars of the last century. You might even catch Eric Clapton or David Bromberg trying out a new ax. Umanov also has an excellent repair staff for taking the dings out of your old Sears Silvertone.

It's not unusual to see a line snaking along in front of Cucina Stagionale, 275 Bleecker Street. Prices are rock-bottom at this Northern Italian eatery, the food is well-prepared, and they don't take reservations, so lines form almost nightly at this popular restaurant.

Lines are common, too, across the street at John's Pizza, 278 Bleecker Street, whose phenomenal reputation has permitted this pizzeria to expand into four storefronts along the street. They even sell John's T-shirts. Whether the pizza is as good as it was back in 1934 when John's opened is another matter. Partisans on both sides of the question will loudly defend their positions. In any case, "No slices" is the rule. Table service or take away.

Caffè Vivaldi, 32 Jones Street, is a neighborhood coffeehouse with a warm, inviting look that includes a crackling fire in the fireplace on cold winter days. Espresso, cappuccino, assorted coffees and teas, pastries, and light bites are the fare.

Nostalgia for old-time toys brings in browsers (and buyers) to Second Childhood, 283 Bleecker Street. Metal trucks, toy soldiers, dollhouse furniture, farm animals, old advertising signs, and even old-time drugstore products make up this fascinating, almost museum-like store.

Ottomanelli's Meat Market, 285 Bleecker Street, is the Village's version of a small-town butcher. Many customers are hailed by name, and everyone looks forward to the excitement of winter holiday food preparation when Ottomanelli's puts up their huge wall-sized list of names for turkey and game orders.

Greenwich House, a block from Sheridan Square at 27 Barrow Street, is a pioneering neighborhood settlement house founded in 1901 by Mary Kingsbury Simkhovitch. Inspired by the example of Chicago's Hull House, she targeted the slum areas around Jones Street as a base of operations. Well-bred and college educated, she fit the profile of the young, urban idealist attracted to settlement work as a career at the turn of the century. As the head of Greenwich House, Simkhovitch devoted herself to serving the immigrant poor and improving their lives in America. Commenting on the gentrification of the Village, she said: "It was certainly . . . astounding to us who had fought against cellar lodgings as unhealthful, damp, and unfit for human habitation, to see them revived as 'one room studios' and rented at six times the original rate." She was ninety when she died in 1957.

The **Ridiculous Theatrical Company** at The Charles Ludlum Theatre at 1 Sheridan Square exists, says its director Everett Quinton, to "counter theatre that has become so tame and safe. We believe that the audience needs to be on edge and enjoy experiment." Carrying on the tone set by its late founder, Charles Ludlum, the troupe is known for its original, campy, and farcical productions, and celebrated its twenty-fifth anniversary in 1991. One of the company's classic works, *Bluebeard,* is Charles Ludlum's portrayal of a baron insistent on creating a third sex. *The Bells* is a one-man, one-hour bit of late-night madness that

Charles Ludlum at a Westbeth rehearsal, March 23, 1972

has been adapted by Everett Quinton. The Ridiculous Theatrical Company cast has included Eureka, Bill Graber, Lisa Herbold, H. M. Koutoukas, Jim Lamb, Stephen Pell, Quinton, and Kevin Scullin.

Directly across from the theatre is Boxer's, a rousing, jumping college-type saloon with Tiffany lamps and checkerboard tablecloths. Giant pitchers of beer seem to be on every table.

West 4th Street from Sheridan Square to Sixth Avenue presents an assortment of tourist arts-and-crafts shops, jewelry shops, boutiques, and some good bars and restaurants that really come alive at night. During the quiet 1950s The Circle-in-the-Square theatre was on 4th and Barrow Streets as well as Louis's Tavern, one of the best-known literary bars in Greenwich Village. Both institutions were replaced with an ugly modern apartment building. Nevertheless, 4th Street is still a major attraction with much to see and much to do. Facing the handsomely landscaped triangle-shaped community garden is the Ridiculous Theatrical Company.

MacDougal Street

MacDougal Street; Coffeehouses; The San Remo; Maxwell Bodenheim; Minetta Tavern; Joe Gould; Folk Music: Phil Ochs and Bob Dylan; Speakeasy; The Liberal Club; Polly's Restaurant; Washington Square Book Shop; Provincetown Playhouse; John Barrymore

MacDougal Street, together with West 3rd, 4th, and Bleecker Streets, is the Village that many tourists remember as the most interesting and visually exciting promenade, night or day. Here is the largest concentration of espresso cafés, pizzerias, taverns, arts-and-crafts shops, restaurants, theatres, and off-beat clothing and souvenir shops to be found anywhere. On MacDougal Street, you can see a parade of the latest fashions in Village makeup, clothing, and accessories. For many years, stripjoints flourished along West 3rd Street; none remain today. Instead a proliferation of coffeehouses and jazz and rock cabarets dominate the district's entertainment scene.

The coffeehouses began with the opening of Edgar's Hobby and David's in the late '40s. These pioneered the espresso café catering to the young Bohemian, hip-college, folk music/chess generation settling in the Village. In 1955 came The Figaro, The Caricature, and The Rienzi. Their successful operation as European-type coffeehouses, where for the price of a cup of coffee you could sit for hours reading foreign newspapers provided by the management, playing chess, or visiting with friends, led the way for an astonishing number

62

of others, some situated side-by-side. In the late 1950s a new onslaught of cafés opened: The Fat Black Pussy Cat, Dragon's Den, Washburn's Thirdside, The Bizarre, and Why Not? A whole new generation was attracted to the cafés, for unlike bars and nightclubs, there was no liquor and no minimum age requirement.

Diane diPrima performs at the Gaslight Café, June 28, 1959

The popularity of the Beat Generation poets inspired coffeehouse poetry readings to add to the continental atmosphere. Appearing in the coffeehouses—mostly in the Gaslight Café and Café Bizarre—were the brightest lights of the Beat Generation, including Jack Kerouac, Allen Ginsberg, Gregory Corso, LeRoi Jones, Ray Bremser, Ted Joans, Taylor Mead, Diane diPrima, Frank O'Hara, Jack Micheline, Tuli Kupferberg, Howard Hart, William Morris, Dan Propper, Hugh Romney (aka Wavey Gravey), and scores of others. Poetry readings in cafés were swiftly followed by folk and chamber-music concerts, pantomime acts, sex lectures, political discussions, Chaplin films, improvisations, and one-act, two-act, and three-act plays. As the '60s drew to a close, most of the coffeehouses faded away. By 1969, when the Café Figaro (on the corner of Bleecker and MacDougal Streets) closed, after the demise of many of its peers, it seemed as though the coffeehouse phenomenon had run out of steam forever.

But a walk around the Village today proves the coffeehouse has come full circle: cozy, relaxed European-style cafés, complete with Italian and French espresso specialties, abound. Caffè Vivaldi, the Cornelia Street Café, Reggio, Dante, Lucca, Artisti, and even a Café Figaro reincarnated on the same corner of Bleecker and MacDougal where the original Figaro stood are there for a new generation addicted to café au lait and good conversation.

The social life of the Village centered on two MacDougal Street restaurant/bars after World War II, Minetta's Tavern and the San Remo (which closed in the 1980s). Other popular neighborhood drinking spots like The Square Bar, MacDougal's, Terry's, The Bat, and The Pony Stable attracted ex-GIs and '40s bopsters and hipsters.

The **San Remo**, 93 MacDougal Street (northwest corner of Bleecker Street), became famous as a rendezvous of Village Existentialists. Many writers, from James Baldwin and James Agee to Michael Harrington, frequented the bar. It was also a favorite haunt of the brilliant, doomed poet **Maxwell Bodenheim**, who went from bar to bar selling or trading his poems for the price of something to eat or a drink. Those who bought his scribbled poetry found it more doggerel than verse. His favorite epigram was "Greenwich Village is the Coney Island of the soul." Along with fellow members of "The Ravens" poetry group, he hung his poems on a fence during the Outdoor Art Shows.

Bodenheim, the author of fourteen novels, was one of the most colorful figures in Chicago from 1913 to 1923, before he came to the Village. His Village escapades, love affairs, and scandalous pranks made international headlines. One involved a commercial artist, Virginia Drew, who sought Bodenheim's advice for her poetry and novels. Bodenheim read them with her, called them sentimental trash, and proudly pointed to his own best-selling novel, *Replenishing Jessica,* as an example of good writing. Drew cried and said that if she couldn't write like Bodenheim she would commit suicide. In the morning she was found floating in the East River. Bodenheim's life came to a tragic end in 1954 when he and his wife, Ruth Fagin, were shot and stabbed to death by a maniac in a five-dollar-a-week room on the Bowery.

The **Minetta Tavern**, 113 MacDougal Street, with its famous backroom murals depicting the early days of the Village, was the favorite hangout of the late **Joseph Ferdinand (Professor Seagull) Gould**, a bearded, bald-headed eccentric 1911 Harvard graduate who always smoked his cigarette in a holder held with thumb and forefinger, palm up. Minetta's is still going strong in the '90s.

In 1920, Gould came to New York and worked briefly as a police reporter for the *Evening Mail*. For many years, he literally shuffled about the Village writing down in notebooks, diaries, or on wrapping paper his monumental *Oral History of the World,* a collection of conversations and observations that he started in 1917. It contained detailed life stories of characters he met on park benches, in bars, Bowery flophouses, public library reading rooms, anywhere he encountered an opportunity to record his scene.

Joe Gould (Professor Seagull) at the Minetta Tavern, early 1950s

Although not a panhandler, Gould, in exchange for a drink, would flap his arms and caw like a seagull; this unusual behavior earned him the nickname Professor Seagull. He often ate the crusts nature-lovers tossed out to the birds. He was the author of the famous lines, "In the winter I'm a Buddhist/In the summer I'm a nudist." When Gould vanished from the Village scene in the '50s, it was rumored that he had inherited millions and retired to his native Norwood, Massachusetts. The truth was that he had become ill. He was taken to Columbus Hospital, turned over to Bellevue, and finally committed to Pilgrim State Hospital for the mentally ill in Brentwood, Long Island. Joe Gould died at the age of sixty-eight in 1958, the last of the 1920s Village Bohemians. His unpublished manuscripts in cheap ten-cent notebooks, said to total ten million words, were lost or scattered to the winds. Some may have been given to his friends, like artist Harold Anton, writer Malcolm Cowley, poet e. e. cummings, photographer Aaron Siskind, or Eddie Sieveri, owner of the Minetta Tavern.

Many people's image of Greenwich Village in the '60s is forever linked with the intertwined trio of MacDougal Street, folk music, and Beat poetry. John Mitchell's famous Gaslight Café, located at 116 MacDougal Street, was a gathering place for Beats and the site of many poetry readings, as well as a venue for standup comics like Bill Cosby and a legion of folksingers. Other clubs were Gerde's Folk City, the Bitter End, the Night Owl, and the Thirdside; favorite hangouts included Izzy Young's Folklore Center, the Kettle of Fish bar, and, of course, Washington Square Park, where it seemed everyone who was anyone, or wanted to become someone, came on Sunday afternoon.

Bob Dylan wasn't the first, or the only, singer to come to MacDougal Street to seek his fortune, just the most famous. Phil Ochs, Dave Van Ronk, Tom Paxton, Pete Seeger, Arlo Guthrie, Buffy

Sainte-Marie, Len Chandler, John Lee Hooker, Joan Baez, and Peter Yarrow, [Noel] Paul Stookey, and Mary Travers (aka Peter, Paul, and Mary), and hundreds of others played on MacDougal Street early in their careers.

In the early 1960s, two folk giants, **Phil Ochs** and **Bob Dylan**, arrived on the scene. It was a combination of their attitudes, their music, lyrics, and lives that propelled them to star status among folk fans and their professional performing colleagues. In the summer of 1963, the folk-music movement moved from cult to mainstream status with the first Newport Folk Festival. It was a successful mix of folk, bluegrass, gospel, jazz, and ballads with musicians like Ochs, Paxton, and the now-household names of Dylan, Seeger, and Baez.

When he arrived in Greenwich Village, Bob Dylan was fresh from The 10 O'Clock Scholar, a Minneapolis coffeehouse (he was born Robert Allen Zimmerman on May 24, 1941 in Duluth, Minnesota and raised in the nearby mining town of Hibbing); Ochs's previous stop on the folk trail was Farragher's Bar in Cleveland. Philip David Ochs was born on December 19, 1940 in El Paso, Texas. Their careers started on a parallel track, but continued in wildly different ways.

Both were drawn to New York for the same reason—to make beautiful protest music. Ochs, who received his high-school diploma at a ceremony hosted by conservative senator Barry Goldwater, took up singing after he was refused the editorship of a college humor magazine. Preferring to be called a topical singer rather than a folksinger, Ochs took his songs from the news stories of the day. His music, expressing the '60s generation's distrust of the establishment and the government's disastrous handling of the Vietnam conflict, was a seminal element in America's growing antiwar movement. His own cynicism and despair is brilliantly portrayed in his second album *I Ain't Marchin' Anymore,* which described the seeming futility of war.

Although Ochs enjoyed great popularity on the Village club scene, none of his albums sold very well. Through time he supported various causes, organizing a benefit for Chilean refugees and a big Central Park concert when the Vietnam war ended. But Ochs never achieved first-rank status in the industry, support among the public, or satisfaction in his personal life. On April 9, 1976, he hanged himself at his sister's house in Queens.

Dylan, meanwhile, for the incalculable, intangible factors that make one person a star and another not, was rocketing to fame. His early pieces, like "Blowin' in the Wind" and "Masters of War" were extraordinarily influential from the earliest days of the peace and civil-rights movements. Followed by his fans through extreme changes in his ever-evolving style—beginning with his use of an electric guitar in 1965—his music achieved dizzying heights of popularity. But he literally had a crash along the way: His 1966 motorcycle accident put his career on hold, but not his fame.

Phil Ochs on MacDougal Street in front of Café Feenjon, January 3, 1965

After recovering from his accident, Dylan continued his chameleon-like changes, emerging as a country-rock star on *Nashville Skyline;* a confessional singer/songwriter on *Blood on the Tracks;* a born-again Christian rocker on *Slow Train A'Comin';* and, most recently, a self-parodying singer-in-disguise as a member of the supergroup, the Traveling Wilburys. During his career, Dylan has performed in support of many causes: for Amnesty International, Live Aid, Farm Aid, Artists United Against Apartheid, and at the George Harrison concert for Bangladesh. Always an enigmatic figure personally, his albums still make the charts, his national and world tours are headline news, he has received numerous awards including France's highest cultural honor, a Grammy lifetime achievement award, and has been inducted into the Rock and Roll Hall of Fame, and he has even opened a baby-clothes store in Hollywood with his cousin, called "Forever Young" (in honor of one of his more popular songs).

Speakeasy, 107 MacDougal Street (at Bleecker Street), began its life about a decade ago as the latest in the great tradition of Village folk-music clubs. It is located on the site of the old Rienzi Café. For a time, it was the home base of New York's *Fast Folk* magazine and musicians' cooperative, which spawned such diverse talents as Suzanne Vega, Jack Hardy, and Shawn Colvin. The club still has an open-mike night where you can hear sensitive guitar strummers, but the professional acts now tend toward the progressive rock end of the musical spectrum.

The **Liberal Club**, founded in 1913 at 137 MacDougal Street, combined the functions of a pub, art gallery, dancehall, gaming room, and laboratory theatre for neighborhood intellectuals. It was to be a "meeting place for those interested in new ideas." The Club sponsored an amazing variety of off-beat programs running the gamut from discussions of the tango and the fad for slit skirts to imagist poetry and left-wing politics. Henrietta Rodman was a typically idealistic member—she crusaded for women's suffrage, cut off her hair and went hatless, and advocated free love.

Bob Dylan's first appearance in New York in February 1961 at the Café Wha with Karen Dalton (cntr) and Fred Neil (r)

In 1915 a number of the Club's regulars—director Lawrence Langner, scenic designer Robert Edmond Jones, and Helen Westley— formed a group called the Washington Square Players, which, after a few successful seasons, moved uptown in 1919 and became the Theater Guild. Among others who came to the Club were authors Sherwood Anderson, Louis Untermeyer, Vachel Lindsay, Max Eastman, and Floyd Dell.

Conveniently located right below the club, **Polly's Restaurant** was a cozy retreat for hungry intellectuals. Anarchist Polly Holladay staffed her little café with radicals and served cheap meals to her Bohemian customers. House chef and waiter Hippolyte Havel set the tone in Polly's by heaping abuse on unlucky diners, whom he loudly denounced as "bourgeois pigs." This MacDougal Street eatery was the first of three Village locations for Polly's, later at West 4th Street and Sheridan Square.

The **Washington Square Book Shop**, 135 MacDougal Street, was next door to the Liberal Club and Polly's. Founded and managed by Charles and Albert Boni, it was the center of Village literary life and offered titles on such radical topics as sex and birth control. Around 1914, the wall separating the bookstore from the adjoining Liberal Club was broken through, but literature sales did not increase. Impoverished intellectuals simply picked up books from this easily available source, read them, and then returned the volumes into stock—thus leaving the store with a supply of rather used-looking books. By 1918, the store moved to 27 West 8th Street, in the building with *The Little Review*. The Boni name became part of book-publishing history when the brothers began publishing books under their own imprint. They soon joined forces with Horace Liveright to form Boni & Liveright, one of the forerunners of the modern publishing giant Random House.

The story of the **Provincetown Playhouse** at 139 MacDougal Street, includes some of the greatest names in Village lore— playwright Eugene O'Neill and poets Edna St. Vincent Millay and e.e. cummings—and goes back to 1915, when a group of vacationing Villagers on Cape Cod were producing one-act dramas on their porch. George Cram "Jig" Cook and his wife Susan Glaspell took over a creaky Provincetown wharf where they first produced the work of the then unknown young O'Neill. His *Bound East for Cardiff,* a short but touching drama about a dying seaman, was an immediate success. In the winter of 1916, the Wharf Theater Group, renaming themselves the Provincetown Players, moved into the parlor floor of a brownstone next door to the Liberal Club and Polly's. Space was tight, and, in 1918, the Players moved three doors south. Rent was $400 a month for the property that had been built as a riding stable. A fundraising campaign helped defray the costs for conversion into a legitimate theatre with a stage, houselights, and benches seating 184.

The theatre continued to produce most of O'Neill's output from the late teens through the 1920s. His stark, brooding work (*The Hairy Ape, The Long Voyage Home*) departed sharply from the light plots that dominated American theatre and reflected his private anguish and desire to reveal the raw truth of life. "I have never written anything which did not come directly or indirectly from some event or impression of my own," he said. His plays often portrayed characters from the Village's radical fringe and barrooms that he frequented.

Edna St. Vincent Millay joined the troupe in answer to a casting call for an ingenue to perform in Floyd Dell's *The Angel Intrudes.* Other early productions of the Provincetown Playhouse included Susan Glaspell's *Close the Book* and *Trifles,* Maxwell Bodenheim's *The Gentle Furniture Shop,* and Alfred Kreymborg's Dadaist farce, *Lima Beans.* Miriam Hopkins and Bette Davis also worked there. Probably the most controversial play was James Light's staging of e. e. cummings's expressionist drama *Him,* which opened on April 18, 1928. The play as written contained twenty-one scenes, 105 characters, and many difficult scene changes. With the author's consent the cast was reduced to thirty, and ingenious staging made the play easier to follow. Critic Alexander Woollcott and columnist Walter Winchell called *Him* pretentious claptrap. Edmund Wilson and Stark Young rose to its defense. The ensuing publicity filled the Playhouse, although it is questionable how many of the audience understood the drama.

The Provincetown Playhouse no longer enjoys its avant-garde reputation of the '20s. The theatre, now called simply the Province-town, is still used by Village companies, none of which has been able to recreate the theatre's past glory.

John Barrymore was a long-time Village resident. Before his stage successes, Barrymore's famous profile was a familiar sight at the

Maxwell Bodenheim evicted from his apartment at 163 Bleecker Street for back rent, 1952

old Brevoort Hotel, where he was usually the center of a boisterous party. With his acting triumphs came an avalanche of intrusions on his privacy by female theatregoers. To escape their oppressive attentions he wanted a "hideaway that would please a nun's grandfather," and he retreated to a penthouse studio at 104 West 4th Street in 1917.

Barrymore decorated his apartment lavishly with Chinese gold wallpaper and exotic furniture. He converted his roof into a pleasure dome covered with thirty-five tons of rich soil hoisted up by block and tackle. He planted a lawn on the roof, and built a winding stone staircase leading to a nautical penthouse complete with ship's wheel and bell. Soon the roof began to cave in by slow degrees, muddy water oozed down the golden walls, and officials of the Buildings Department began to harass him about the numerous violations. Barrymore's response was to abandon his apartment and Greenwich Village.

When Barrymore died in 1942 at the age of sixty, a tall tale circulated that his body was stolen from the funeral parlor by his actor pals Errol Flynn and W. C. Fields. Supposedly, they took it to Barrymore's home, where they propped it up in a club chair and threw a huge drunken party in Barrymore's honor. When the party was over, they simply returned the stiff for burial. Dead or alive, John Barrymore was always the life of the party, so to speak.

The West Village/Sheridan Square

The West Village; Gay Street; Northern Dispensary; Sheridan Square; Stonewall Inn; Julius's Tavern; Oscar Wilde Book Store; Lion's Head; Tom Paine House Site; Piano Bars; Condomania; James Agee; Sweet Basil; St. John's Evangelical Church; White Horse Tavern — Dylan Thomas, Norman Mailer; Westbeth — Merce Cunningham, Erick Hawkins

In 1806, the Common Council commissioners zoned the Village's thinly settled area east of Sixth Avenue into a latticework of neatly squared streets. But the more densely settled West Village, with its curving and swerving thoroughfares, was too well-established to be changed. Leaving this charming section just as they found it, the commissioners continued uptown, doggedly zoning the unsettled countryside into a monotonous grid pattern.

As a result, the West Village is today at odds with the rest of New York. For example, West 4th Street jogs uptown and to the right, intersecting 10th, 11th, and 12th Streets before terminating at 13th Street. In addition, Waverly Place changes direction abruptly, and the street signs can give visitors the illusion that there are two Waverly Places that intersect each other. Even Villagers have difficulty finding their way around the West Village.

Along with their unique patterns, many West Village streets today retain their original cobblestone paving. Still lining the old-fashioned byways are many of the Federal-style houses built in the

73

early 19th century. With such reminders of the area's past days as a country village as the charming enclave dominated by the spire of St. Luke's Church, the Greek Revival row houses on Barrow Street, and quaint Grove Court, visitors have little trouble stepping back in time as they stroll the picturesque West Village streets.

Gay Street, a stable alley that evolved into a byway of modest row houses in the 1840s, is a half block from Sixth Avenue, is only a block long, and curves sharply from Christopher Street to Waverly Place. It has beautiful Federal style houses that are over 150 years old. It officially opened in 1833 according to Common Council minutes, and was long the home of African-American families, many of whom were employed as servants for the gentry of Washington Square. The area degenerated into a ghetto, and was not revitalized until the 1920s.

During prohibition, many of the Gay Street buildings housed speakeasies. This picturesque block was portrayed by Ruth McKenney in her popular book *My Sister Eileen* (later made into a movie) and the musical *Wonderful Town,* based on her adventures while living in the basement of 14 Gay Street. Mary McCarthy, after separating from her first husband, lived at 18 Gay Street. McCarthy was a noted essayist and novelist, famous for her polemical points-of-view.

The **Northern Dispensary**, a curious three-sided brick building, fills a triangular island at the junction of Christopher and Grove Streets, where Waverly Place divides and runs along two of the building's sides. When it was built in 1831, the Dispensary was at the northernmost limit of New York, hence the name. The clinic was founded in 1827 by local citizens to provide health care for the poor of their locality. An early record of the clinic indicates that Edgar Allan Poe was treated here for a head cold in 1837, the same year he brought his thirteen-year-old bride to New York. Poe occupied the house at 85 West 3rd Street during 1845 at the height of his

The Northern Dispensary

career. While living there he published his spectacularly successful poem "The Raven." Before moving to 3rd Street, Poe lived first at 113 Carmine Street and later at 137 Waverly Place, near the Dispensary.

Other names associated with the Northern Dispensary include author Artemus Ward and singer Jenny Lind. Townsend Harris, America's first Ambassador to Japan, chaired its annual meeting of 1866. The clinic offered dental care until the late 1980s, when the building was totally refurbished in line with community plans to convert it into a facility for AIDS patients.

Sheridan Square, at the intersection of Grove, Christopher, Washington Place, Seventh Avenue South, and West 4th Street, is the focal point for tourist night life in the West Village. Day trippers from New Jersey, Long Island, and the outer boroughs arrive on the subway and by bus, taxi, and car to visit some of the best night spots in the Village. The Square is named for General Philip Sheridan, a Union officer in the Civil War, and his statue dominates the small park on the Square. During the Civil War, Sheridan Square was the scene of the bloody draft riots, which were in protest of the Enrollment Act passed to force New York State to contribute its full quota of men to the war effort. When the provost marshall tried to enforce the draft, mobs of men and women overpowered the police, and looted, burned, and killed for three days. African-Americans and Irish protesters suffered the most during the riots, and the owner of the old house that stood at 92 Grove Street hid some of them under his building to save them from being hung by the mob. The Burges Chamber Studios, now occupying the site, was the first studio apartment house built in the Village and its design was awarded a first prize by the American Institute of Architects.

The events of the night of Friday, June 27, 1969 at the **Stonewall Inn,** 51 Christopher Street (at Sheridan Square), have been termed a gay Boston Tea Party, a turning point in the lives of gays and lesbians in the U.S., and perhaps most cogently, the birth of the gay civil-rights movement. As is true for most such seminal events, the night began unremarkably with just another police raid on a gay bar, the Stonewall. But this raid was different than earlier ones—instead of meekly walking into the police wagons as they were taken out of the bar, the bar patrons resisted arrest. Other gays and lesbians poured out of nearby bars and shouted encouragement to their friends. Words turned into actions, beer bottles were thrown, someone dislodged a parking meter and used it as a battering ram on the bar door, and others rocked the patrol wagons. The first of several nights of defiance had begun.

First gay pride demonstration, after the Stonewall Riots, on Christopher Street, July 27, 1969

According to police records, that June 27th raid was a routine action in search of "illegal liquor sales." To gays in the dance bar, it was the usual police harassment of a gay gathering place. But this raid was to be anything but routine. The next night the Stonewall remained closed, but an even larger crowd gathered on Sheridan Square to confront the police. A number of people were hurt, including both civilians and police officers, but there is no doubt the riots galvanized gay political and social activity and became a rallying symbol of the gay movement.

The annual gay pride marches throughout the U.S. held in June commemorate the Stonewall Riot, but it seems premature to say that antigay prejudice has disappeared: The owner of the building housing the bar refused to allow a commemorative plaque to be put up. However, the city of New York has renamed that block of Christopher Street "Stonewall Place." After the Stonewall closed, several businesses, including a bagel restaurant, have occupied the space. After years of discussion, a George Segal sculpture was installed in Sheridan Square Park in 1992 to commemorate the riots and honor the role that gays and lesbians have played in Village life.

Three years before the Stonewall Riots, another gay-rights milestone took place on April 21, 1966, when four members of the first gay men's group, the Mattachine Society, staged a "sip-in" at Julius's Tavern, 159 West 10th Street. Dick Leitch, John Timmons, Randy Wicker, and Craig Rodwell stood at the bar and told the bartender they were homosexuals. Service was denied on the grounds that it was illegal to serve homosexuals, and the men left the premises. Ironically, years later Julius's became a gay bar.

The pioneering **Oscar Wilde Bookshop,** 15 Christopher Street (at Gay Street, near the site of the Old Stonewall Inn), was founded by Craig Rodwell and carries a complete selection of books on gay and lesbian concerns.

The **Lion's Head,** 59 Christopher Street (on Sheridan Square, near Seventh Avenue South), dubbed "The Last Great Saloon" by *Vanity Fair* magazine, celebrated its silver anniversary on January 14, 1991. Affectionately known as the Head to the legions of journalists, writers, actors, and artists who make up the saloon's family of regulars, the bar is owned and operated by Judy and Wes Joice.

The entrance is a few steps down from street level. Once inside the warm and cozy barroom, visitors have no trouble identifying this as a home away from home, with its wood-paneled walls, decently dim lighting, and book jackets by authors Stanley Crouch, Cynthia Heimel, Nicholas Pileggi, Mike McAlary, and Lucian Truscott IV framed on the wall. The bar has an adjoining dining room, with well-spaced tables, and the food is surprisingly good, going way beyond traditional pub grub for excellent lunch and dinner offerings.

The Lion's Head, then at the corner of Charles and Hudson Streets, was opened by Leon Siedel, as a traditional coffeehouse/ restaurant. It became a popular oasis, with no music or entertainment, to relax over coffee and a newspaper or eat an inexpensive dinner. When the restaurant moved to its present location, in the 1960s, the *Village Voice* was also on Sheridan Square, at the corner of Christopher Street and Seventh Avenue South, and many *Voice* writers frequented the Head, among them Joe Flaherty, poet Joel Oppenheimer, and social commentator and author Michael Harrington.

Over the years, a list of personalities who have frequented the Lion's Head includes columnists Pete Hamill and Nat Hentoff; authors David Markson and Sid Zion; Feminist writers Susan Brownmiller and Kate Millett; newspaper reporters Mike Pearl, Timothy McDarrah, and Vic Ziegel; actors Ally Sheedy, Timothy Hutton, Matthew Broderick, and Al Pacino; activist/politician Bella Abzug; and TV newscasters John Miller and Mike Taibbi.

The site of the **Tom Paine House,** 59 Grove Street (at Seventh Avenue South) is marked by a brass plaque. Paine, the author of *Common Sense, The Crisis,* and *The Rights of Man* lived here at the time of his death in 1809. Born in England the son of a Quaker

77

George Segal sculpture memorializing the Stonewall Riots, Sheridan Square Park, July 1992

corsetmaker in 1737, Thomas Paine was a jack of all trades engaged in a variety of occupations when he came to America in 1774. His eloquent writings on behalf of republican government and independence have become part of our ideological heritage. He began his *Crisis* papers with these famous words: "These are the times that try men's souls. The summer soldier and the sunshine patriot will, in this crisis, shrink from the service of their country." Paine joined the Revolutionary army and his writings helped strengthen the resolve of many who enlisted in the fight for independence.

Paine's Village sojourn, which began in July 1808, was not a happy one. Many Villagers denounced him as an atheist and infidel and demanded that he embrace an orthodox religion. Paine refused to do so but did request that he be buried in a Quaker graveyard, a request that was refused.

There are four piano bars on and around Sheridan Square. Marie's Crisis, 59 Grove Street, has had a piano player tickling the ivories for over fifty years, playing a mixture of jazz, show tunes, and popular songs. The club's name derives from its first owner, Marie Dumont, and the fact that Thomas Paine, the American Revolutionary author of the *Crisis,* once lived on this site.

At Arthur's Tavern, 57 Grove Street, a bar wraps around the piano and musician's area where music of the '30s and '40s is heard from 8 PM till 1 AM. The Duplex Cabaret, next to the Lion's Head at 61 Christopher Street, is on the corner formerly occupied by the *Village Voice.* One of New York's longest-running cabarets, the Duplex features comedy and music revues. Joan Rivers, Woody Allen, Dick Cavett, and Jerry Stiller and Anne Meara all performed here in the 1960s. A long tradition of audience participation makes the Duplex one of the city's most enjoyable nightspots. The Five Oaks, 49 Grove Street, features jazz and Broadway melodies in a laid-back, simpatico setting.

Near Sheridan Square at 351 Bleecker Street is one of Greenwich Village's newest, most essential, and amusing retail stores, **Condomania.** Created in the age of AIDS, it is the brainchild of Adam Glickman and Suzy Landolphi who know that safe sex sells. The store is jammed with every known brand, size, and style of condom for giants or midgets. Among its bestsellers are Glow-in-the-Dark condoms, mint-flavored condoms, and condoms in fortune cookies. The first Condomania store opened in the Village in 1991; by the end of 1992, there will be twelve Condomania shops nationwide with estimated sales over one million dollars. As the guidebooks say, worth a visit.

According to Susan Edmiston and Linda Cirino's *Literary New York,* poet/novelist/film critic/screenwriter **James Agee** came to the Village in 1932, renting a basement apartment at 38 Perry Street. He later moved to a walkup apartment at 172 Bleecker Street, but he had to abandon this home after suffering a heart attack in 1951. For the last four years of his life, he lived in a house at 17 King Street. Agee could often be seen drinking alone at the San Remo, the popular literary bar, in the '40s and '50s.

Agee was born in Knoxville, Tennessee. After graduating from Harvard, he wrote for several magazines. His Depression study of Alabama sharecroppers, rejected by *Fortune* magazine that had originally commissioned it, was published along with Walker Evans's photos in the classic book *Let Us Now Praise Famous Men.* As a literary celebrity he went to Hollywood and wrote screenplays for *The*

Village Cigars, Sheridan Square

African Queen and *The Night of the Hunter*. His only novel, *A Death in the Family*, was awarded a posthumous Pulitzer Prize. Agee's letters to Father James H. Flye, an Episcopal priest at St. Luke's on Hudson Street and his old schoolteacher and lifelong mentor, were published in 1962.

Sweet Basil, 88 Seventh Avenue South near Bleecker Street, presents a mixture of jazz styles, from New Orleans to modern. Among their top acts are The Eddie Chamblee Quartet; trumpeters Doc Cheatham and Terumasu Hino (the Miles Davis of Japan); the McCoy Tyner trio; the Toshiko Akiyoshi Quintet; the Art Farmer Quintet; Joe Beck and Red Mitchell; the Tommy Flannigan Trio; the Nat Adderly Quintet; and the music of Gil Evans played under the direction of his son, Miles Evans.

St. John's Evangelical Church, 81 Christopher Street, is a handsome Federal-style church that was built in 1821–22 as the Eighth Presbyterian Church. The church is set back slightly from the building line of the adjacent structures on the street, and features a completely symmetrical facade. Three round-arched doorways with deep paneled reveals give access to the church through double doors with semicircular glass transoms above. Three arched windows above these doors are set between fluted pilasters that begin at sill level and extend up to the cornice where they meet the ends of the large triangular pediment.

The church was organized in 1819 and S. N. Rowan, D.D., was installed as pastor in the same year, serving until 1830. In 1842, the church changed denominations and became St. Matthew (P.E.) Church, an acquisition made possible through gifts by the estates of Charles Morgan and Thomas Otis. It was consecrated in March 1842 and Rev. Jesse Pound was made the new Rector. In 1858 it became St. John's Lutheran Church.

The **White Horse Tavern**, 567 Hudson Street (at West 11th Street), became a literary shrine when the famous Welsh poet Dylan Thomas made it his second home in the 1950s. The bar now features wall-to-wall murals of the poet. On his first day in New York, February 21, 1950, Dylan Thomas was taken to Greenwich Village by his host, John Malcolm Brinnin, and introduced to Julian's Bar, the San Remo, the Minetta Tavern, and, on a later trip, to the White Horse, where he was greeted by Ernie Woltzheimer, the congenial proprietor who slid a Scotch down the bar to him. Ernie always drank with his favorite customers.

Dylan Thomas is best known for his long poem, *Under Milk Wood,* describing a day's activities in a small seacoast village in Wales. Thomas read it with a full cast of players at the 92nd Street YW-YMHA on May 14, 1953. I remember it as an electrifying experience.

In the early 1950s, The White Horse joined the San Remo, Minetta's, and Louis's Tavern on Sheridan Square as favorite literary hangouts. Writers Michael Harrington, Dan Wakefield, and David Markson were the first to discover the Horse's unique charms in 1951. Markson in turn introduced Brinnin and Thomas to the pub. During the day it was an Irish longshoreman's bar, but at

Delmore Schwartz in the back room of the White Horse Tavern, February 22, 1959

night the regulars showed up at 11 PM. Harrington and his friends (who worked on text and reference books during the day) arrived an hour later. Everybody stayed until the bar closed.

Norman Mailer, representing an entirely different literary group, began Sunday afternoon social gatherings at the White Horse. Among those who came were Daniel Wolf and Ed Fancher (who founded the *Village Voice* in October 1955 with Mailer). There was a reluctance to attend formal salons, but in the course of its existence various writers showed up: Vance Bourjaily, Hortense Calisher, Louis Auchincloss, Cyrilly Abels, Calder Willingham, John Maloney, William Styron, Sigrid deLima, Herman Wouk, James Jones, Lewis Allen, and Frederic Morton (who drank only ginger ale). The Sunday meetings frequently ended with bitching about publishers, but perhaps the idea for the 1952 anthology *Discovery* edited by Bourjaily and John Aldridge resulted from these White Horse gatherings.

Westbeth, 463 West Street, occupies a square block from Bank to Bethune Streets, extending west to Washington Street; the entrance courtyard faces Bank Street. Before its conversion into cooperative housing for artists, the rambling white building was used as a research facility for Bell Laboratories. The conversion was undertaken by the philanthropic Kaplan Foundation under the aegis of Joan Davidson. The building is now home to the studios of numerous painters, sculptors, photographers, and performance artists like choreographer and dancer Merce Cunningham, founder of the Merce Cunningham Dance Company.

The Company began in 1953 when Cunningham, once a dancer with Martha Graham, took a troupe of dancers to Black Mountain College, a progressive liberal-arts school in North Carolina, to rehearse a repertory of dances that were to be presented in New York City. Incorporating a Zen-derived, untitled, unstructured theory devised by John Cage, the original dancers included the musician David Tudor and the painter Robert Rauschenberg, as well as Carolyn Brown, Viola Farber, Remy Charlip, and Paul Taylor, all of whom have gone on to become choreographers in their own right.

Fresh with success in New York, the Merce Cunningham Dance Company toured the Far East, India, and Europe through the '50s and '60s, garnering praise and recognition from audiences, but they were regarded as perverse, frivolous, and irrelevant by the "dance establishment." Soon, dancers began to flock to Cunningham's

Carolyn Brown and Merce Cunningham in How to Pass, Kick, Fall and Run
(1966 performance)

classes to learn his technique, which was fast becoming a viable instrument for dancers of all persuasions and not just a vehicle for Cunningham's particular point of view.

From the '60s through today, Cunningham has collaborated with many talents including artists Jasper Johns, Frank Stella, Andy Warhol, Robert Morris, Mark Lancaster, William Anastasi, and Dove Bradshaw. More recently he has been exploring the possibilities of choreographing for the camera ("videodance" and "filmdance") with Charles Atlas and Elliot Caplan in coproductions with broadcasters in Britain (the BBC), France (La Sept), and PBS. "With the death of George Balanchine," wrote the *Wall Street Journal* in 1985, "it has become very clear that Merce Cunningham now stands alone as the dominant artistic force in American dance."

Erick Hawkins Dance Company was formed by one of the greats of modern dance, who has expanded from his Greenwich Village roots to international recognition. For many years, Hawkins's studio was located on Bethune Street, near Westbeth. A master choreographer, Hawkins is known for dances that avoid linear or literal interpretations and seek a more poetic element with metaphor and symbol. His works often incorporate the avant-garde compositions of Lucia Dlugoszewski, whose music makes use of many nontraditional sounds (paper, combs, even silence). Hawkins's dance company's performances in New York City are usually held at the Joyce Theatre, 175 Eighth Avenue (at 19th Street), a performance space that is home to many of the City's finest dance companies. Hawkins current studio is housed in 38 E. 19th Street (off Fifth Avenue), a building that is also home to the José Limón company.

South Village/Bedford Street

Samuel Whittemore House; Bedford Street; Grove Street; Twin Peaks; William F. Hyde House; Grove Court; The Church of St. Luke's in the Fields; Lucille Lortel Theatre; Lee Chumley's; Cherry Lane Theatre; Twin Houses; The Narrowest House in New York; St. Luke's Place; Film Forum 2/Le Cinematographe; S.O.B.s; Edna St. Vincent Millay House; Richmond Hill Site; The New York Fire Museum

The **Samuel Whittemore House**, 45 Grove Street (at Bleecker Street) was built in 1830, and was once a free-standing mansion, surrounded by spacious grounds with its own cistern, well, hot house, and stables. It was undoubtedly one of the finest and largest Federal-style residences in Greenwich Village. The scale of the house, over forty-seven feet in width, reflects the importance of the man for whom it was built. Together with other members of his family, Whittemore was one of the largest property owners in the Village. He was the manufacturer of steam-propelled carding equipment used in the textile industry, for which his older brother, Amos, had taken out a patent in 1797. Samuel Whittemore was a long-time resident of the Village; in 1811, he served as an election inspector and, in 1816, he served as State Assemblyman. In the 1820s, he was among those landowners who were most active in the laying out and paving of streets in this area of Greenwich Village.

Bedford Street, between Morton and Commerce Streets, boasts several of the oldest houses in the Village. Historically, it is important because much of this property once belonged to Aaron Burr. The street was laid out prior to 1799 and was named after a street in London. Three charming old brick-fronted residences dating back to 1821 are located at 64–68 Bedford. A distinctive row of Greek Revival town houses at numbers 65–75 dates back to 1830. At 77 Bedford (corner Commerce Street) is the oldest existing house in the Village, known as the Isaacs-Hendricks House. It was built for Joshua Isaacs, a merchant, in 1799–1800, but he was not the owner for long; Isaacs lost the property to his creditors and it was purchased by his son-in-law Harmon Hendricks in 1801. Harmon Hendricks had a copper mill in New Jersey, and he and his brother-in-law Solomon Isaacs were the New York agents for silversmith Paul Revere, founder of the copper-roller industry in the U.S. (and best known for his midnight ride to warn his countrymen that the British were coming!)

Grove Street, west of Bedford to Hudson Street, offers a delightful vista. Facing west, there is St. Luke's Chapel, which serves historically and visually as a focal point at the end of the street. On the left are two fine rows of late Federal-style and Greek Revival houses, separated by Grove Court, a quiet oasis behind the busy streets that surround it.

Twin Peaks, 102 Bedford Street (at Grove Street), is an architectural curiosity, a small building with two steep roofs. Originally built about 1830 as a two-and-a-half-story frame house with dormers, it was totally redone in 1925 by Clifford Reed Daily, with the financial backing of the banker and art patron Otto Kahn. According to local legend, the architect wanted to make it an "inspiring home for creative workers." It is now a five-story stucco building adorned with pseudo-medieval half-timbering. Bay windows project from the front of the building and are framed by half-timbering.

Adjoining Twin Peaks, at 100 Bedford, is the little 1833 building that once housed the shop of a sashmaker, William F. Hyde. His residence was next door, at the corner of Grove and Bedford Streets, and is now called by his name, the **William F. Hyde House,** 17 Grove Street. This charming clapboard house, built in 1822, is a vivid reminder of 19th-century Village life, although some architectural historians decry its 1988 restoration, saying it existed only briefly as it is today. Historians feel that only the left-hand side of the house was

Grove Court Entrance

built prior to 1822, and the right was added later to fill in an existing yard. Whether or not it is authentic to its original look, the building adds a picturesque aspect to this historic street.

Grove Court, one of the Village's many exclusive courtyards, opens onto the graceful bend in Grove Street between Hudson and Bedford Streets. The Court, which is entered through a gate wedged between numbers 10 and 12 Grove Street, is lined with small houses dating from the 1830s. These fine brick-fronted three-story buildings were planned for workingmen. The court was known as Mixed Ale Alley in the 19th century, perhaps a reference to its occupants' drinking habits. By the early 20th century, it was called Pig's Alley, before the courtyard as a whole underwent a facelift, with the picturesque addition of decorative shutters, entrance porches, and garden plots, and the single-family dwellings were converted into apartments. A locked cast iron gate keeps the court private, but passersby can still have a satisfying peek at this charming byway.

The Church of St. Luke's in the Fields, 479–485 Hudson Street (at Grove Street), was built in 1821 as an uptown chapel of Trinity

William Hyde House and Twin Peaks

Parish. Set back from the street behind an iron fence, the charming little country church is flanked by uniform rows of town houses, with trees introducing a bit of green. It is the third oldest church building still in use in Manhattan (preceded by St. Paul's Chapel downtown and St. Marks-in-the-Bouwerie in the East Village). It was called St. Luke's in the Fields because there were no other buildings near it except the Amos farmhouse and Brant Tavern at Spring and Hudson Streets. "City" people coming to the cornerstone-laying ceremonies arrived by sailboat on the river, then much nearer to the church, or crossed over the canal (now Canal Street) via Broadway or Greenwich Street. There were two stagecoaches a day then between the City and the Village.

The church owns the entire city block on which it stands and is responsible for the recent rehabilitation of the old buildings on it. It is a unique example of extremely tasteful block planning, which retains the beauty of its early Federal architecture and yet converts the area to modern needs. In the 1840s, St. Luke's Parish House was the boyhood home of Bret Harte, author of *The Luck of Roaring Camp*. Years later

88

Harte became a thorn in the side of his Village neighbor and fellow literary giant Mark Twain. Harte had insulted Twain's wife, sneered at Twain's house, and borrowed money from Twain without any intention of returning it. Twain never stopped trying to get even with Harte by issuing broadsides in the press.

East of Hudson at 121 Christopher Street is the **Lucille Lortel Theatre**, formerly called the Theatre de Lys. In the 1950s, it was home to a phenomenally successful Marc Blitzstein production of Bertolt Brecht's and Kurt Weill's *Threepenny Opera*. It starred Weill's wife, Lotte Lenya, and the original cast included such young acting comers as Ed Asner, Jerry Orbach, Jerry Stiller, John Astin, and Bea Arthur.

Lee Chumley's at 86 Bedford Street (at Barrow Street) is the only bar and restaurant in New York without an entrance sign. Its past history tells why. Opened in 1928 by Leland Stanford Chumley, who had previously managed a speakeasy on MacDougal Street, the premises at 86 Bedford with its discreet access and ready getaway route proved an ideal location for a speakeasy. Catering to a neighborhood crowd by word-of-mouth, the bar had a furtive alleyway entrance (through an iron gate at 58 Barrow Street into a backyard called Pamela Court) and exit (now the Bedford Street doorway).

The friendly, confidential atmosphere attracted local writers such as John Dos Passos, Theodore Dreiser, and F. Scott Fitzgerald, as well as left-wing radicals, all of whom enjoyed the host's simple cooking, warm fireside, and ongoing games of cards and chess. A colorful border of book jackets of its illustrious patrons—past and present—still paper the wall including Max Eastman's *Marx and Lenin: The Science of Revolution,* Floyd Dell's *An Old Man's Folly,* Edmund Wilson's *Discordant Encounters,* Willa Cather's *The Song of the Lark,* Anaïs Nin's *Little Birds—Erotica,* Djuna Barnes's *Ryder,* and Gloria and Fred McDarrah's *The Artist's World.* Below the jackets are ancient oak booths and wood tables etched with innumerable carved initials. A rare, intact survivor of the Prohibition era, Chumley's is one of the few landmarks with enduring ties to the Village's Bohemian past.

The **Cherry Lane Theatre**, 38 Commerce Street (at Grove Street), was launched in the 1920s by a group of Villagers who envisioned an experimental theatre that would be an alternative to what they considered to be the commercial drift of the established Provincetown Playhouse. They chose for their new theatre an abandoned box factory

St. Luke's Church and Restoration

that had once been a brewery. Many avant-garde productions have been showcased here, notably Samuel Beckett's *Waiting for Godot* and *Endgame,* and contemporary plays by Edward Albee, Jack Richardson, Kenneth Koch, Fernando Arrabal, and Eugene Ionesco.

Twin Houses, 39 and 41 Commerce Street, are two charming little buildings separated by a shared garden. They were built in 1831–32 for Peter Huyler, a milkman. The mansard roofs were an 1870s addition. The "twins" (as they are commonly called) are an interesting combination of late Federal (the brickwork) and French Second Empire (mansard roofs) styles.

The Narrowest House in New York is located at 75-1/2 Bedford Street (at Grove Street). It was built in 1873 and its stepped gable is reminiscent of the Dutch tradition. The half number was probably used to designate half-a-house, because the three-story building is only nine-and-a-half feet wide and thirty feet long. The front of the house actually faces a courtyard, and only the rear is visible from the street. It has been the home of a cobbler and a candy factory. Edna St. Vincent Millay lived here in the 1920s. In recent years, the empty house has deteriorated considerably.

St. Luke's Place, the one-block stretch of Leroy Street that lies between 7th Avenue South and Hudson Street, is a delightful tree-lined street with a long sweep of 1850s Italianate row houses across the street from an open space used as a ball field. The houses have handsome ironwork blending in with vines and various plantings, high stoops, and a spacious outlook. The original owners were all well-to-do merchants. John W. Lewis, a provision merchant, lived at number 2; Matthew Olwell, commission merchant, lived at number 11; and a tailor, William S. Vanderbilt, was the first owner of number 6. William Walker, father of James J. (Jimmy) Walker, the mayor of New York City from 1926 to 1933, purchased number 6 in 1891, and the Walkers owned it until 1934. The two "lamps of honor" on the newel posts, traditional symbols of a mayor's residence, are still there today.

Jimmy Walker was born in 1881 and grew up in the Village. He worked at a variety of jobs—he wrote songs, played semi-pro baseball for Hoboken—before he was elected to the State Assembly in 1909. One of his songs, "Will You Love Me in December as You Do in May?," was a 1908 hit. In 1925 he won the mayoralty race as the Tammany Hall candidate. A witty, glib man and a snappy dresser, Jimmy Walker epitomized the holiday mood of the jazz age, and became a symbol of

5 to 13 St. Luke's Place

good times for the newspapers who considered him the quintessential New Yorker. Although rumors of official corruption and personal indiscretions flew, he seemed immune to criticism. During his first term of office, the parks and transportation system were improved, and his popularity was widespread. But in his second term a legislative investigation led by the noted jurist Samuel Seabury uncovered one million dollars in unaccountable funds in Walker's office. Threatened with dismissal, Walker resigned in 1932. James J. Walker Park, the playing field opposite the family home on St. Luke's Place, is named in his honor.

Other interesting personalities lived in these fine houses. Poet Marianne Moore occupied the basement flat of 14 St. Luke's Place from 1918 to 1929 with her mother and worked across the street at the Hudson Park Branch of the New York Public Library. In 1922 Sherwood Anderson lived in number 12. Theodore Dreiser, who had come to New York in 1895 and lived earlier in a flophouse on Bleecker Street, occupied the parlor floor of 16 St. Luke's Place, where he worked on *An American Tragedy* in 1922 and 1923. Dreiser's 1915 novel *The Genius,* a realistic, semi-autobiographical portrayal of a young, midwestern painter's sexual alliances and infidelities, aroused a storm of criticism for its frankness and inspired the Village literati to battle on behalf of freedom of expression for American writers. By the time he was living on St. Luke's Place, Dreiser's reputation and literary earnings were well-established.

Film Forum 2 at 209 West Houston Street (at Sixth Avenue) boasts three screens and is arguably New York's most prestigious independent and art-film house. Run by Karen Cooper for the last twenty years—the theater has been open for twenty-two—the Film Forum is the place to go to catch your favorite revivals and cutting-edge new films. A short time ago, most titles at the Film Forum might have gone unexhibited if it were not for the Forum's commitment to bringing exotica to the big screen. However, it has paved the way for relative newcomers like the 220-seat Le Cinematographe (15 Vandam Street at Varick Street) run by another dedicated personality, Jackie Raynal-Sarré. Raynal-Sarré began with the (now defunct) Bleecker Street Cinema, and after leaving there in 1990, decided to renovate the old Thalia SoHo revival house and bring another independent-film house to the area. Raynal-Sarré has also installed a twenty-five seat, high-definition video lounge in the basement. Rather than competition, the two film houses see each other as allies, raising interest in their art mediums and providing people with more than one venue to experience them.

If the people who erected the building that houses Le Cinematographe could see it now, they would be profoundly surprised. Built by "Battery Dan" Finn as the Huron Club in 1905, it housed one of Tammany Hall's famous Democratic Clubs of the early part of the 20th Century. The building accommodated the men that controlled New York City politics for fifty years and entertained the likes of Village kingpin Carmine G. Di Sapio, Mayor Jimmy Walker, who

Marianne Moore in the Jefferson Market Library, November 25, 1967

used to conduct his "Court of Appeals" in a smoke-filled room there, and Battery Dan's son, Sheriff Daniel E. Finn, Jr., who also held court here on Monday and Thursday nights. The break was made from political club to theatre in the 1950s when an entrepreneur, Charles Kasher, bought the building for $48,000, converted the first floor into an off-Broadway theatre and the upper two floors into a luxurious duplex. Kasher would rent his 199-seat theatre for $650 a week.

S.O.B.s, 204 Varick Street (at Houston Street) could just as well stand for "South of the Border" as Sounds of Brazil (the club's unabbreviated name), given the panoply of Latin and Caribbean musical styles featured here. Samba, Brazilian acts, reggae, jazz, Caribbean soca, calypso, and salsa bands can be heard here; performers have included Jayne Cortez and the Firespitters; Onaji Allen Gumgs; Israel Vibration; The Mighty Sparrow; Chico Ramos; Bobby Caldwell; Judy Mowatt; Sara Dash and Thuli Dumakude; Charlie Sepulveda Sextet; and Zin and Rara Machine. S.O.B.s is one of the hottest dance clubs around even when the music is not live, which is not often, and there is usually a cover charge on par with the evenings talent; Bahaian dinner is also served.

Another famous figure in Village literary life, **Edna St. Vincent Millay**, lived with her mother and sisters at 25 Charlton Street. Millay began writing poetry during her childhood in Maine and Massachusetts, and in 1912, when she was nineteen, her poem "Renascence" brought her immediate acclaim. To support her writing she worked as an actress and director for the Provincetown Players. Later she was introduced by Edmund Wilson to the editor of *Vanity Fair,* Frank Crowninshield, who brought her work to a wide public. Millay wrote plays, including *Aria da Capo,* but is best remembered for such poetry as "First Fig," beginning with the famous lines: "My candle burns at both ends;/ It will not last the night. . . ."

In 1921 Millay went to Paris on assignment for *Vanity Fair*. She returned in 1923, the year she won a Pulitzer Prize in poetry, and married Eugen Boissevain. They lived for a short time at 75½ Bedford Street, moved to Steepletop, a farm in Austerlitz, New York, and then she set out on a reading tour of the Orient, never again to return to Greenwich Village.

Richmond Hill, a luxurious mansion and country retreat, once stood on the land now known as the Charlton-King-Vandam Historic District (at Sixth Avenue). An English paymaster, Major Abraham Mortier, built the great mansion in 1767. At that time, the hilltop site commanded a panoramic view of New Jersey. Here George Washington planned the strategy for his Long Island campaign in April 1776, and later Vice President and Mrs. John Adams lived here when New York was the nation's capital. Aaron Burr leased the estate from Trinity Parish from 1794 to 1804; he counted as guests French statesmen Elie Charles de Talleyrand and Louis Philippe, American politicians Thomas Jefferson, James Madison, and Alexander Hamilton, and the social and political aristocracy of the country. After his notorious duel with his erstwhile guest Hamilton in July 1804 in Weehawken, New Jersey, Burr was indicted for murder and fled to Philadelphia.

In 1817 John Jacob Astor took over the Richmond Hill property, now divided into lots. When the city commissioners in their 1811 plan laid out a street plan that included leveling Manhattan to its present flatness, the mansion was literally rolled down to the southeast corner of Charlton and Varick Streets. The lots were sold off, and most of the houses built there in the 1820s and 1830s, notably 23–29 Charlton

Street and 48–50 King Street, survive today. The mansion became a tavern, then in 1831 a theatre, and was finally demolished in 1849.

The New York Fire Museum, at 278 Spring Street (at Varick Street), is filled with steam engines, gooseneck hand pumpers, ladder trucks, tools, uniforms, alarm boxes, hose nozzles, torchlights, axes, rare prints, golden trumpets, collections of medals, trophies, badges, hatchets, fire helmets, and portraits of fire officials and famous fires. All the colorful,

New York City Fire Museum

fascinating apparatus displayed was used in actual fire service. Much of the equipment is unique. A hand-drawn and operated pumper, the Washington No. 1, built in 1820, has a leather hose with seams that are riveted together, a technique similar to that in the sewn hoses used in Holland as early as 1672. The New York Fire Museum is also an educational center on fire prevention and safety.

Soho/West Broadway

Soho Historic District; Picasso *Sylvette* Sculpture; Bookstores; West Broadway Galleries; The Broken Kilometer; The New York Earth Room; Printed Matter Bookstore; A Photographers Place; Shopping/Boutiques; Cafés/Bars; Performance Garage; Nikolais-Murray Louis Dance Company

Transformed in the space of twenty years from a shabby factory district with rusty cast-iron fronted buildings whose lofts were occupied by rag and remnant dealers to an almost oppressively chic environment for art galleries and commerce ranging from haute-couture salons to sidewalk T-shirt vendors, Soho is on everyone's list of top-ten New York sights. It lies just across West Houston Street from Greenwich Village (Soho is an acronym for *So*uth of *Ho*uston). The district's renaissance dates back to the late '50s, when artists began to rent out the factory lofts that made ideal studios for working on the oversized canvases that were then coming into vogue. At that time the district was zoned for commercial use only, and artists who lived in their studios did so illegally.

In the late '60s, pioneering art galleries followed the artists to West Broadway; one of the first was O.K. Harris, now in its second location on the street. More galleries seemed to sprout from thin air, and today the area is chock-a-block full of fine restaurants, cafés, and bars; fashion boutiques; toy, antique, and craft shops; and jewelry, souvenir, and bookstores. Sidewalks are jammed on Saturday afternoons with vendors purveying books and crafts from around the world. Vying for sidewalk space are the hordes of tourists and the locals, the latter usually attired in black, who seem to have enormous patience in sharing their "hot" neighborhood with all comers.

The heart of Soho is the **Historic District**, designated for its wealth of cast-iron buildings, many painted in a pleasing variety of pastel tones, in the area bounded by West Houston Street, Broadway, Canal Street, and Sixth Avenue. This unique concentration of cast-iron buildings goes back to the 1850s, as Broadway slowly began to alter from a street of small brick retail shops into a boulevard of marble, cast-iron, and brownstone commercial palazzos. Lord & Taylor, Arnold Constable & Co., Tiffany, E. V. Haughwout, and other large retailers established their stores on or near Broadway. Major hotels joined them; music halls and theatres opened soon thereafter. The small cobbled streets behind the splendid facades of Broadway became an entertainment center of a different sort—a red-light district. Crosby, Mercer, and Greene Streets, West Broadway, and West Houston Street all had houses of assignation.

As middle-class families left the area, small manufacturing companies moved in, and the second half of the 19th century saw the area develop into a com-mercial center. The most popular styles for these buildings with cast-iron facades, most erected between the 1850s and 1880s, were neo-Grec, French Second Empire, French Renaissance, and Italianate. The streets of Soho are liter-ally lined with cast-iron facades and they are impossible to miss as you stroll. Note that Greene Street, just north of Canal Street, not only has a number of beauties, but the street itself was repaved with cobblestones in 1992, giving it an appropriate period ambience.

Italian tourists being photographed on West Broadway

At the northeast corner of West Houston Street and West Broadway (renamed La Guardia

97

Place north of Houston) stand three thirty-story concrete towers (505 La Guardia Place and 100 and 110 Bleecker Street). A grassy plaza separating the buildings is the site for **Picasso's** *Sylvette,* a thirty-six-foot-high concrete enlargement of the original cubist sculpture. The buildings were designed by I. M. Pei and opened in 1967. A hilarious contrast to the stark modernity of the Pei buildings stands across La Guardia Place—a five-story brick building whimsically painted blue with a cow motif adorning the facade. Bruno's Bakery and Café, 506 La Guardia Place, has outdoor tables that offer a good vantage point to meditate on the contrast offered by this unlikely streetscape.

On the southwest corner of West Houston Street and West Broadway, a popular Italian café and restaurant, Amici Miei, 475 West Broadway, has a fenced-in patio that provides an inviting place to enjoy a meal in good weather. There's indoor seating as well. Another Italian café on the same block, I Trè Merli, 463 West Broadway, has a chic-looking crowd that spills onto the street on balmy days.

Across the street from I Trè Merli is one of Soho's premier bookstores, Rizzoli, 454 West Broadway, a sleek-looking duplex space with an excellent selection of art and architecture books as well as the latest in fiction and nonfiction titles. Spring Street Books, 169 Spring Street (at West Broadway), has (in addition to books) a wonderful selection of magazines from all over the world as well as attractive sale tables that make for good bargain browsing. Japp Reitman Inc., 134 Spring Street (at West Broadway), is one flight up from street level and specializes in art and design books.

But galleries are the principal reason for Soho's fame, and many important venues are on West Broadway, including the internationally renowned Leo Castelli and Sonnabend galleries at number 420. The acknowledged dean of contemporary art dealers, Castelli at the age of eighty-five has been an important force in the career of artists such as Jasper Johns, Donald Judd, Ellsworth Kelly, Joseph Kosuth, Roy Lichtenstein, Claes Oldenburg, Robert Rauschenberg, James Rosenquist, Frank Stella, Cy Twombly, and Andy Warhol.

Other notable galleries in the downtown art world include Barbara Gladstone, 99 Greene Street; Paula Cooper, 149 Wooster Street; Larry Gagosian, 136 Wooster Street; Mary Boone, 417 West Broadway; Nancy Hoffman, 429 West Broadway; O.K. Harris, 383 West Broadway; and John Gibson, 568 Broadway, to name just a few.

Impromptu performance on West Broadway

Many major modern artists since the evolution of the New York School in the mid-1950s through Abstract Expressionism to Pop Art, the New Realism and Post-Modernism have had their work displayed in a West Broadway gallery.

All of the galleries feature changing exhibits, except two, both funded by the Dia Center for the Arts, that display the work of Walter de Maria. One is **The Broken Kilometer**, 393 West Broadway, an extended exhibition, open to the public since 1979: the floor is filled with 500 polished, round solid-brass rods, each measuring two meters in length and five centimeters in diameter. This artwork derives its impact from repetition and the perfection of each rod's exact placement. The other is **The New York Earth Room**, 141 Wooster Street, a must-see. It occupies the entire second floor of a loft building and consists of 250 cubic yards of rich aromatic topsoil piled twenty-two inches deep on 3,600 square feet of floor space. Peace and tranquility pervade the room as the earth seems to absorb all extraneous noise, light, and activity in the space. Visitors are not permitted to walk on the dirt. Both of these displays are like nothing you have ever seen before, and the power each conveys is truly startling.

Printed Matter Bookstore at Dia, 77 Wooster Street (near Spring Street), specializes in artists' works, including flipbooks, bumperstickers, audiocassettes, videotapes, records, and books of all shapes and sizes. Their catalog has an eclectic list of titles, among them a collector's item called *A Cube* by Sol LeWitt that has 511 black-and-white photos representing *every possible combination of nine light sources to illuminate a cube*; a *Fluxus* anthology of music and sound events produced by this ground-breaking art movement of the 1960s; and Leslie Sharpe's *Bra vs. Bra,* a feminist consideration of women's undergarments. Printed Matter also sells Artist's Bookplates (Ex

The Broken Kilometer

Libris) by Francesco Clemente, Robert Gober, Claes Oldenberg, and Nancy Spero in boxed sets.

Harvey Zucker's **A Photographers Place**, 133 Mercer Street (at Spring Street), is the only bookstore in New York solely devoted to photography books. The store carries a large and complete selection of current titles and rare collectors' items, focusing on the work of Paul Strand, Robert Frank, Ansel Adams, Helmut Newton, Mary Ellen Mark, Ralph Gibson, Charleton E. Watkins, Minor White, and Diane Arbus.

If you'd like to buy a work of art, but the budget won't allow a five-figure purchase, stop in at Untitled, the postcard store at 159 Prince Street, for a diverse collection of art-oriented postcards. Rocks in Your Head, 157 Prince Street, sells and buys used compact discs and offers quality bargains. A bargain in dining (take-out only) attracts locals to the M&O Grocery, located at the corner of Thompson and Prince Streets. You can order a substantial hero sandwich, packed with meats and cheeses to your taste, and then have an alfresco lunch nearby at the playground/bocce court/park a block south on Spring and Thompson Streets. Nearby, at 117 Prince Street, is Whole Foods, a natural-foods grocery. It has developed into one of Soho's most popular gathering places, with the sidewalk in front of the store attracting a vibrant lunch-time crowd.

If you're seeking less-casual refreshments, West Broadway restaurants offer good choices. The Spring Street Restaurant and Bar, 162 Spring Street (at West Broadway), serves continental cuisine, and the bar scene is lively as well. Kenn's Broome Street Bar, 363 West Broadway (at Broome Street), is a more down-home spot where you can brunch on salads, burgers, and omelettes or you can stop in anytime for a sandwich and a draft beer. Next door to the Broome Street Bar, the Cupping Room, 359 West Broadway, is a great place to stop in for a cappuccino or a full meal. The atmosphere is country style, with lots of warm wood tones and an old-fashioned air that begins with the lace-curtained front window.

Not too far afield, Fanelli's, 94 Prince Street, is a longtime occupant of the southwest corner at Mercer Street. Originally a local tavern for workers in the nearby lofts, it still offers good-value Italian cooking and an ever-popular bar scene. For light refreshments, Le Petit café, 156 Spring Street (at West Broadway); Dean & DeLuca's café, 121 Prince Street (at Mercer Street); and Café Limor, 303 West Broadway (at Broome Street) are convenient. For shoppers, West Broadway and nearby side streets offer all sorts of treasures. Five Eggs, 436 West Broadway (at Prince Street) has giftware with a

Whole Foods

Japanese theme: kimonos; objects of paper, wood, lacquer, and metal; and jewelry. Fine quality leather wallets and bags are sold at La Bagagerie, 412 West Broadway (at Spring Street). Fashion boutiques such as Harriet Love, 412 West Broadway; French Connection, 435 West Broadway (at Prince Street); and Agnes B, 116 Prince Street (at Greene Street), have cutting-edge designs.

For a bit of fun, there's Think Big, 390 West Broadway (at Spring Street). Enter the land of the big, where familiar everyday products—

1992 Roy Lichtenstein exhibit at the Leo Castelli gallery

office items and school supplies like crayons, pencils, paint brushes, paper clips, and memo pads; toiletries such as toothbrushes and toothpaste; and sporting goods such as soccer balls, tennis balls and racquets, and sneakers—are transformed into gigantic, playful objects. A pocket comb is big enough to rake leaves, the Oreo cookie looks as though it could feed a family of four, and the champagne cork is big enough to be an ice bucket. It's a hoot!

More artistic entertainment is on stage at the **Performance Garage**, 33 Wooster Street (at Broome Street). Founded in 1967 by Richard Schechner, who wanted to open an environmental theatre, it was the first live performance space in the area. The building was originally a metal stamping plant, and when Schechner first took it over, a big garbage truck was parked inside, hence the theatre's name. Outstanding productions have included *Dionysus in 69,* an unusual production of *Makbeth* (sic) that featured a maze that guided spectators through an historical tour of earlier *Macbeth* productions, and works by Sam Shepard, Jean Genet, and Bertolt Brecht. Monologuist Spalding Gray began public showings here in the mid-1980s. Today, the resident company called the Wooster Group, directed by Elizabeth LeCompte who took over from Schechner in 1980, continues to offer stimulating and offbeat events. Among its famous alumni is actor Willem DaFoe.

The fifth floor of 375 West Broadway is home to the **Nikolais-Murray Louis Dance Company** and studio. Alwin Nikolais is one of the pioneers of modern dance, one of the first to create "total" theatrical events melding lights, costumes, sound, and movement. He was director of the Henry Street Playhouse school and company on the Lower East Side from 1948 to 1968. Murray Louis, who for many years was the lead dancer in the Nikolais company, began creating his own dance solos in the '50s. Besides creating choreography of great wit and feeling, Louis has become one of the leading dance educators in the country. The two companies joined forces in the late '80s and now share one of the Village's most vital and important dance spaces. Students come to study here year round from all over the world.

Tribeca/Greenwich Street

Tony Smith's Smug; Wetlands; Roulette Music Loft; Walkers Bar; Soho Photo; Sufi Books; Artist's Space; Franklin Furnace; Matthew Brady; Chanterelle Restaurant/New York Mercantile Exchange; Bubby's; Tribeca Film Center; Harrison Houses

A tour of Tribeca (the *Tri*angle *Be*low *Ca*nal) begins at Varick and Laight Streets near the exit of the Holland Tunnel. In the huge open plaza is a black crab-like monster constructed of wood that measures eleven feet high by eighty feet long and seventy feet wide. This public sculpture is **Tony Smith's Smug** project underwritten by the famous Paula Cooper Gallery in Soho. The sculpture was intended to be made in steel, but Smug was never fabricated nor publicly exhibited during Tony Smith's lifetime. It was first built in the artist's backyard in Orange, New Jersey in 1973. Both the original and current mock-up were made out of plywood and employ hinges to join the sculpture's triangular faces into a lattice of regular and stretched octahedra.

Peace-love-and-happiness might be the mantra of another era, but it still rings true at **Wetlands**, 161 Hudson Street (at Laight Street, three blocks below Canal). This nuclear-free, biodegradable, vegetarian nightclub features only PC (politically correct) patrons and acts. It is probably the only club in the world that uses a VW microbus as the souvenir shop. This is the place to hear the latest in Hippie music and to relive the glory days of the '60s.

Tony Smith's Smug

Roulette Music Loft, 228 West Broadway (at White Street), occupies a loft designed especially for musical events. Founded in 1978 by its current directors, Jim Staley and David Weinstein, Roulette offers a professional concert setting for new works by composers and mixed-media collaborators. Young musicians as well as established avant-garde composers perform their own works; nearly all the concerts feature world premieres. The broad range of musical genres represented include contemporary, new jazz, electronic and computer music, experimental rock, audio art, and homemade instruments.

Walkers Bar, 16 North Moore Street (at West Broadway), is one of the most delightful places in Tribeca to have lunch or just meet a friend for a drink. With its pressed tin ceiling, old-fashioned tile floor, exposed brick walls, and carved wood bar, Walkers provides a comfortable setting to pig out on grilled chicken with crispy french fries for less than ten bucks. Guinness on tap is a house specialty. Walkers has been a bar since 1890 when the Washington Market was a major food-distribution center.

Soho Photo, 15 White Street (at West Broadway), is the oldest cooperative photo showcase in New York. Founded in 1971 by two

New York Times photographers, Lee Romero and Donal Holway, it now has over 100 members of varied interests and talents whose work encompasses a broad spectrum of original styles: photo-documentary journalism hangs near abstract and conceptual art photos, large color prints, hand-colored works, and manipulated Polaroid images. The gallery is located in a former warehouse where eggs were stored. The space has been renovated and now includes a balcony guest-exhibition area and a downstairs gallery that can accommodate four solo exhibits, three smaller shows, and a group show.

One Saturday each month, the work of prospective members is screened at the gallery. In addition to its primary mission of exhibitions, the gallery fosters a sense of community for photographers with a program of lectures and workshops. Thousands of amateur and professional photographers have exhibited here, among them Minor White, Eva Rubinstein, and Max Waldman. I had the inaugural exhibition there in January 1971. David Chalk, a professional photographer, has been managing the gallery for over ten years.

Sufi Books, 227 West Broadway (at White Street), is an unusual and interesting outlet for those who want books on Sufism. If this is an unfamiliar subject, the bookshop offers this explanation:

> Sufism is the subtle unfolding of the esoteric teachings of Islam, the exploration of the precise relationship of man to the Divine. The Sufi Path embraces the intense longing for genuine mystical experience, that longing which turns the attention of sincere spiritual seekers within as they seek an inner path towards the Divine.
>
> Sufi Books specializes in exploring the fullest range of Sufi teachings including the poetry of the inspired Sufi poets (Rumi, Ansari), biographies of Sufi saints (Ibn Ata Illah, Ibn Abbas of Ronda), writings of the classic Sufi masters of esoteric thought (Ibn Arabi, Sharafuddin Maneri), and a rich selection of the teachings of current Sufi masters and schools of Sufi training (Sheikh Muzaffer, Javad Nurbakhsh, Sheikh Nazim).

Artist's Space, 223 West Broadway (at White Street), no stranger to controversy both in its funding and in its exhibitions, continues to be synonymous with support for artists at crucial stages in their careers. Its mission is to translate that legacy into an ongoing, tangible reality. As a broad-based culture center, Artist's Space aggressively pursues its role to seek out and to develop new projects that explore a variety of issues and ideas in all forms of expression.

Franklin Furnace, 112 Franklin Street (at West Broadway), is a museum for multiple art published after 1960: artists' books and magazines, audio art, mail art, Fluxus works, posters, videotapes, and films. Franklin Furnace also houses a library of reference works on historical and contemporary avant-garde movements and an archive of unique documents, such as correspondence, notebooks, and slides from artists.

Created by artist Martha Wilson in 1976, Franklin Furnace now has the largest collection of its kind in the United States with over 18,000 works, including books by Claes Oldenburg, John Baldessari, Alice Aycock, Sol LeWitt, Ida Appelbroog, Ed Ruscha, Jenny Holzer, Barbara Kruger, and Joseph Beuys. Books are housed in 100 percent acid-free archival enclosures stacked in steel bins in the gallery. Any book in the collection is available to anyone who wants to read it.

Franklin Furnace has been one of this city's genuinely experimental alternative spaces. Martha Wilson believes that "time" is the artistic medium of the 20th century and, in keeping with this concept, has initiated artists' readings and performances with such name brands as avant-garde performers Laurie Anderson, Vito Acconci, Richard Artschwager, Dara Birnbaum, Les Levine, Robert Morris, Holly Hughes, Carolee Schneemann, and William Wegman. Controversial performers Eric Bogosian, Karen Finley, Holly Hughes, Donna Henes, Michael Smith, Paul Zaloom, and Theodora Skipitares all made their first public appearances in the basement of Franklin Furnace.

Going east across Franklin Street to Broadway there are two landmarks of special interest: 359 and 361 Broadway. In 1881, W. Wheeler Smith designed 361 Broadway, a monumental cast-iron building. Both the Franklin Street and the Broadway facade stand as they were built with only a slight alteration to the front entrance. The large sheets of glass in the windows indicate how far American glass technology had advanced by 1880. The architect incorporated different facade details at each floor level such as vine, leaf, and spiral designs, and geometric fluted and banding designs. Many of the iron front buildings with large glazed openings were provided with rolling iron shutters to be pulled down at night, a common custom all over

New York. But the shutters on this building long ago have rusted in the up position and do not function anymore.

359 Broadway, home to Matthew Brady's second photography studio

In 1853 Matthew Brady opened up his second photography gallery over a saloon at 359 Broadway. His first gallery was at 207 Broadway with an entrance at 162 Fulton Street. In 1844, Brady became instantly successful as a photographer; this was only five years after the introduction of the Daguerreotype. In 1860, Brady moved again to the southwest corner of Broadway at 10th Street across from A. T. Stewart's Dry Goods Store (later Wanamaker's). Brady's gallery reflected wealth and good taste, appropriate for America's premier photographer. His floors were covered with velvet tapestry, the ceilings were painted with frescoes, lace curtains covered the windows, and on the walls were Brady's masterful portraits of generals, kings, heads of state, and presidents. When Brady was interviewed in 1891 by a New York *World* reporter, he said when he "took Mr. Lincoln in 1859 he had no beard, I had to pull up his shirt and coat collar; that was at the Tenth Street gallery." (Brady got his dates wrong.) Two years later, Lincoln said "Brady and the Cooper Union speech made me President of the United States." Brady went bankrupt in 1873 and died in the pauper's ward of New York Presbyterian Hospital.

The **Chanterelle Restaurant**, 2 Harrison Street (at Hudson Street), is one of Tribeca's swankiest eateries. Like the great restaurants of France, it is owned by a husband-and-wife team, chef David Waltuck and maitress d'hotel Karen Waltuck, who personally oversee this elegant room, with oversized bay windows, a pressed tin ceiling, and magnificent flower arrangements. The cuisine is on the highest level, with the best of ingredients employed in an innovative menu highlighting classic French dishes as well as Far Eastern flavors. Their signature dish is grilled seafood sausage, studded with pine nuts and sauced with a beurre blanc. A typical dinner choice might begin with squab mousse with green peppercorns, then continue with an entree of salmon with garlic confit, and conclude with strawberry-rhubarb shortcake. Both lunch and dinner menus change monthly. Their wine cellar boasts some 3,000 bottles, not including the cognacs, Armagnacs, port, and dessert wines.

Originally located in Soho, the Chanterelle moved in 1989 to its current location, the grand, 19th-century New York Mercantile Exchange building, a Queen Anne/Romanesque revival brick-and-granite landmark constructed in 1885 by the architect Thomas R. Jackson who designed many other buildings in lower Manhattan. The Exchange began in 1872 when a group of dairy merchants banded together as the Butter and Cheese Exchange of New York, in an effort to improve the organization of the trade of their goods. They intended to create a centralized location for the pricing, selling, and distribution of their products, something that had previously been accomplished with other commodities. By 1880, the group had become the Butter, Cheese, and Egg Exchange of New York, and in 1882 the organization changed its name to the New York Mercantile Exchange,

Walker's Bar

expanding their roster to include the grocery, dried fruits, canned goods, and poultry trades.

Bubby's, 120 Hudson Street (at North Moore Street), is an unpretentious eatery popular for breakfast and lunch. It features the rough, unfinished look. The place is small, intimate, and is in a bright corner location so it is lively and cheerful. Its menu is avant-garde cuisine, which means mussel stew, grilled fresh turkey on sourdough bread, broiled squid and scallions in ginger sauce, linguine with toasted pecans, huge salads, and grilled tofu sandwiches can all be found on a day's menu. The menu, which leans toward the healthy and accommodates vegetarians, does not feature beer or wine. Bubby's is a comfortable place that gives a new twist on classic items.

The **Tribeca Film Center**, 375 Greenwich Street (at Franklin Street) is the inspiration of actor, director, and producer Robert De Niro, who sought a place where film people could conduct meetings, screen their films, eat with other film people, and generally cut down on overhead by sharing costs. There did not seem to be any places where people in the film industry could meet each other casually, get together for some fun, or talk business. When the Martinson Coffee Company warehouse, a 1905 landmark, became available, De Niro's idea became a reality and (after some interior renovations) the Tribeca Film Center opened in 1989.

On the street level is the Tribeca Grill, one of the hottest eateries in which to be seen, which is not too hard because the entire corner of the restaurant is walled by large glass windows. Although everyone comes for the food, some customers hope they will run into ballet superstar Mikhail Baryshnikov, or actors Bill Murray, Ed Harris, Christopher Walken, or De Niro himself.

The second floor has a banquet and meeting room, common kitchens, and New York's premier, state-of-the-art commercial screening room that can be rented by professionals as well as the general public. The room seats over seventy-two in luxurious comfort and is equipped with two 35-mm interlocking projectors. The screening room also boasts the unique Lucasfilm's THX sound technology offering superior sound quality to any other facility in the City.

Miramax Films, the trend setting independent, foreign, and art-film distributor occupies the entire third floor. Founded in 1979 by native New Yorkers Harvey and Bob Weinstein, Miramax has released some of the most critically acclaimed and commercially successful films, including *The Grifters,* Madonna's concert documentary *Truth or Dare, Scandal,* and *Cinema Paradiso.* The documentary *The Thin Blue Line* was instrumental in freeing Randall Adams from jail; *Pellé the Conqueror* won the 1991 Academy Award for Best Foreign Language Film; *sex lies and videotape* won the prestigious Palme d'Or at the 1991 Cannes Film Festival; *My Left Foot* was named 1990's Best Picture by the New York Film Critics Circle and won two Academy awards.

"King Anthracite," an environment by Stashu Kybartas, depicting the struggle of Pennsylvania's coal miners, at Artist's Space

The other floors in the Tribeca Film Center house New York headquarters for producers Stephen Spielberg, Ron Howard, the Hudlin Brothers and Quincy Jones, the Black Filmmakers' Foundation, literary agent Jack Tantleff, Art Linson Productions, *Screen International* (a film-trade magazine based in London), and First Look, a joint project of Eastman Kodak, the Tribeca Film Center, and the New York Foundation for the Arts, which is a monthly showcase for independent films that are screened for industry executives, distributors, exhibitors, producers, and agents. Tribeca Productions, run by Robert De Niro and Jane Rosenthal, is in the penthouse; De Niro's office comes complete with its own Jacuzzi, a steam room, and a 1,000-pound coffee scale.

The main advantage offered by the Tribeca Film Center is not the amenities, but that transient professional film people who come to New York to make a film can rent offices on a temporary basis and take advantage of the many facilities that the center can offer and thereby cut total overhead. Producers who have used Tribeca's facilities include Mario Van Peebles (*New Jack City*), Fred Caruso (*Bonfire of the Vanities*), and Eddie Murphy (*Boomerang*).

At Greenwich and Harrison Streets are the **Harrison Houses,** a group of nine restored Federal-style family homes. Six of the houses survive in their original locations. Three others have been moved from nearby streets. The earliest of the group dates from 1796. Two were designed by John McComb, Jr., New York's first native-born architect, who lived in one of them for many years. They were originally built for people of considerable means and were intended to be discreet and unpretentious. When the Washington Market moved to the Bronx, these houses were abandoned, and through the efforts of the Landmark's Preservation Commission, were restored and sold to homeowners. This unique group of homes is dwarfed by the towers of Independence Plaza to the south.

Canal Street

On April 14, 1804, the City Council approved the construction of a canal to run from the freshwater pond north of Foley Square to the Hudson River. Complete with a promenade and the Old Stone Bridge that spanned the water at Broadway, the canal was the northern end of New York City. Ten years later, with the City exploding North, it was decided that the land was too valuable, and the canal was filled and the Old Stone Bridge buried!

Dramatic physical alterations to Greenwich Village after 1917 eroded the insularity it had long enjoyed from the rest of Manhattan. The cutting through of Seventh Avenue South below Greenwich Avenue after World War I, the opening of Sixth Avenue below Carmine Street in the 1920s, and the new subways that attended these developments greatly improved access to and from the neighborhood. The completion of the **Holland Tunnel** in 1927 created a vehicular link between New York's west side and New Jersey that heightened the area's use as a traffic corridor. These commuter conveniences left irreparable scars on the Village landscape, however, and increased the intrusive presence of tourists and transients.

All along Canal Street, from end to end, you can feel and hear the thunder and roar of huge ten-ton trucks that make it the most

Canal Street traffic jam

traffic-clogged thoroughfare in the area. When the Holland Tunnel opened on November 13, 1927, Canal Street became one of New York's most air-polluted routes. Burrowing under the Hudson to New Jersey on the west, the Tunnel, along with the Manhattan Bridge that spans the East River to Brooklyn on the east, created a direct, convenient route for trucks to slice through Manhattan. Besides all the traffic, the streets are always jammed with people, because Canal Street is the home of the bargain. Canal Street shops spill their merchandise in bins all over the sidewalks: hardware, electronics, plastics, wood, stereos, file cabinets, decrepit used clothing, and numerous geegaws that defy description: no one really knows what they're for. Many of these so-called bargain stores carry much of the same merchandise.

The unifying element of Canal Street is its old-world, outdoor market/bazaar atmosphere. Many of the merchants are ethnic vendors who sell merchandise of their native lands. There are some special places like **Pearl Paint** housed in a dilapidated loft at 308 Canal (at Broadway). This artists' mecca caters to the professional and casually creative and stocks everything from portfolios to inexpensive portable watercolor sets.

114

If you visit Pearl Paint, don't miss the many other unusual retailers between Broadway and Wooster Street. You can buy wholesale sheets of colored plastics at Industrial Plastics, 309 Canal Street, or be awed by the variety of rubber tubing available at Canal Rubber, 329 Canal Street, or return to the world of plastic buttons at Canal Plastics, 345 Canal Street. Customers in these crowded stores include everyone from conceptual artists searching for that elusive item to complete a sculpture to plumbers looking for a washer to repair a faucet.

The most fascinating store on the street, **Canal Hardware**, 305 Canal Street, is filled to the rafters with an astonishing selection of monkey wrenches, ratchet sets, pulley assemblies, micrometers, hammers, Allen wrenches, wood planes, bubble levels, and hacksaws. Power tools are a specialty here with a profusion of drills, sanders, and routers. For "real men" or women, too (who may eat quiche but also do repairs), from house wreckers to house builders, this store is paradise.

Double-parked cars are lined up with their trunks open as mechanics perform Canal Street's famous ritual of installing awesome car stereos at **Canal Audio** (353 Canal Street at Wooster Street). Packing 250-watt amplifiers in the trunk with speakers everywhere, these systems can be heard throughout the City, thumping ear-deafening tunes while their drivers wait at red lights. They give out earplugs with every system installed!

The truly adventurous may want to explore the **Lower East Side**. Although many consider this neighborhood a slum (at best), it has many streets that are slowly being gentrified, while it continues to absorb new immigrants from Puerto Rico, Cuba, Haiti, the Dominican Republic, and Jamaica. Between 1846 and 1860, two million Irish migrated from their famine-stricken country and settled in the Lower East Side. The mid-19th century saw a major immigration from Germany. In 1881, the great influx of Mediterranean and Eastern Europeans to the United States brought Italians, Greeks, Turks, Russians, Rumanians, Slovaks, and Poles into the area.

Between 1881 and 1910, a million-and-a-half Jews emigrated to the Lower East Side, to form the world's largest Jewish community. The memory of this teeming Jewish community has been honored in such award-winning films as *Hester Street* and *Enemies: A Love Story,* both filmed on location on the Lower East Side. Lower East Side tenements housed the growing population of new immigrants.

Orchard Street in the 1950s

Quotas established in the early 1920s slowed the area's growth, and, in 1934, the first public housing in the city was built to replace the deteriorating tenements. Many old buildings survive, and one has even been made into a museum.

The Lower East Side Tenement Museum, 97 Orchard Street (at Broome Street), documents that unique period in the history of nearly every immigrant group when it first called New York City home. What is a tenement? Simply, a dumbbell-shaped, brick apartment building, six stories high, on a twenty-five-foot-wide lot. On each floor there were usually four "railroad" apartments (from front to rear, each room opens onto the next, linked like the cars of a railroad train). The bathtub was in the kitchen, and the community pull-chain toilet in the hall, one per floor. Many tenements were abandoned, then torn down, as a result of the 1935 City ordinance requiring a toilet in every apartment. The museum tells its story with living

Roof-top gathering, the Lower East Side

dioramas: in a gloomy second-floor walkup, an elderly German seamstress works by gaslight, sewing clothing for her children. Down the hall, a Chinese laundry worker is scrubbing clothes. The exhibits in the 1868 building also portray an Italian, an African-American, and a Hispanic family.

Broadway

Canal Jean; Broadway Panhandler; French Culinary Institute; E. V. Haughwout Building; Singer Building; Dean & Deluca; The Guggenheim Museum in Soho; The New Museum of Contemporary Art; The Cable Building; Pfaff's Beer Hall; Tower Records/Tower Books; NYU Tisch School of the Arts; Astor Place Hair Designers International; Grace Episcopal Church; Strand Book Store; Forbidden Planet

Broadway is the longest boulevard in New York. Its diversity is remarkable, exhibiting a complete cross-section of cultural, financial, ethnic, and artistic styles and tastes from beginning to end. Broadway lost its residential flavor in the 1840s when many of the inhabitable buildings were converted to commercial use. As described by Margot Gayle, author of the authoritative *Cast Iron Architecture in New York,* cast iron was widely used on these commercial buildings because relatively few, slender columns were needed to support facades; therefore, big windows were possible. In the days before electric light, these large windows allowed for natural light to pour into the commercial work spaces. Cast-iron columns also allowed for soaring ceilings and barn-like floor spaces capable of accommodating large machinery and many workers. Architecturally speaking, cast iron's greatest advantage is that it can be easily adorned with intricate architectural detail, manufactured cheaply, and quickly shipped and installed. James Bogardus, who created and patented machinery for constructing prefabricated, mass-produced iron-building parts, was instrumental in promoting this revolutionary building component; he also invented a new method for printing postage stamps.

Broadway has more famous cast-iron landmarks than any other single street in New York. From Canal Street to Astor Place, there appears to be very little architectural change since the turn of the century. The retail stores in the area sell fabrics, antique furniture, used clothing, kitchen supplies, and there is even a lumberyard. In the 1980s, Broadway became saturated with art galleries as Soho and its art community spilled east. Some buildings have as many as a dozen galleries, which makes it quite convenient for culture seekers.

At the corner of Howard Street is a five-story handsome cast-iron structure with eighteen arched windows. Thomas R. Jackson completed this building two years after one of his other great works, The New York Mercantile Exchange, further south at Harrison and Greenwich Streets.

Canal Jean, 504 Broadway near Spring Street, never uses the expressions "used clothes" or "previously owned garments," but they built their reputation on decent previously owned and recycled clothing. Situated in one of the classic cast-iron buildings of 1860,

Hari Krishna street vendors in front of Tower Records

119

Canal Jean enjoys six bays that are treated in two-story units; two-story columns separate each vertical window group with rounded upper windows. The ground-floor storefront was crafted at Daniel Badger's Architectural Iron Works on 13th and 14th Streets between Avenues A and B. Badger's catalog from 1865, which illustrates complete facades, describes this design as "spermcandle style."

There are all kinds of interesting cookware, including a good selection of the Le Creuset line, at **Broadway Panhandler,** 520 Broadway (at Spring Street), and the store offers discounts on most items ranging from 15 to 40 percent off what you'd find anywhere else in the City. Amateur and professional bakers know the Panhandler as a prime source for pastry-making and cake-decorating equipment. Dishes, decorative tableware, and table linens round out the offerings.

New York City's preeminent center for professional instruction in the culinary arts, the **French Culinary Institute,** housed in a building with two addresses, 462 Broadway and 120 Grand Street, offers price-fixed meals prepared by the next generation of great chefs. An impressive corner building that has been covered with unsightly marble on its Broadway face, 462 was designed by John Correja in 1879 and is a massive example of the many cast-iron commercial palaces designed in French Renaissance style. Its six stories are combined into a total of twelve bays on the Broadway side and twenty-four bays on the Grand Street side.

Richard Morris Hunt, America's first Paris-trained architect, identified with millionaire mansions and the Metropolitan Museum of Art, designed 478 Broadway in 1874. Hunt was also the architect for the Lenox Library, Boston's Fogg Museum, the [Chicago] *Tribune* Building, as well as Marble House and the Breakers in Newport, Rhode Island. In this instance, Hunt broke away from his customary imitation of stone and created 478 Broadway with iron for iron's sake. All five floors have simple rectangular windows divided by the slenderest of columns, which are grouped into three wide bays. This building has survived much as Hunt originally conceived it, including the ground floor, a rarity considering the ever-evolving tastes of storefront retailers. Ground-floor pilasters carry a circular shield bearing the street-address numerals. The structure was built as an investment by Roosevelt Hospital, which had inherited the property from its founder and benefactor, James H. Roosevelt, whose law office and residence were here from 1843 to 1861.

The **E. V. Haughwout Building**, 488 Broadway, designated a New York City Landmark on November 23, 1964, is on the National Register of Historic Places, and is the most celebrated cast-iron building still standing in New York. All of its finely cast details are still intact, including the original clock face. Designed by Brooklyn architect John Gaynor, 488 was completed in 1857 using components from Badger's Architectural Iron Works. Built expressly for Edgar V. Haughwout, a merchant in cut glass, silverware, clocks, and chandeliers, the building was meant to convey the significance of the operation that supplied chinaware to the White House. Five stories high, nine bays wide on Broadway and fourteen bays wide on Broome Street, this colossal building displays Venetian Renaissance characteristics. The basic window unit is repeated ninety-two times on the Broadway and Broome Street facades. Although passenger elevators had been used earlier, the first truly practical one with automatic safety devices was designed by Elisha Graves Otis and installed in the Haughwout building. The building is now occupied by a mill outlet selling cotton goods.

The **Singer Building**, 561 Broadway (at Prince Street), was designed by Ernest Flagg in 1904 for the Singer Sewing Machine Company. This twelve-story office and loft building incorporates a distinguished facade of colored terra-cotta, glass, and lavishly decorated wrought-iron balconies.

Dean & DeLuca, 560 Broadway (at Prince Street), is a mecca for food connoisseurs, its stark white walls the perfect backdrop for the brilliant colors of the foods and kitchenware on display. A small espresso bar at the entrance adjoins the pastry and cake department, and it's hard to resist buying a sweet treat to eat with your coffee. Luscious displays beckon throughout the store: the cheese department has items from around the world, including English Stilton, French Chevre, Italian Gorgonzola, and New York State cheddar. Smoked salmon, vegetarian and meat patés, onion and cheese tarts, and black and green olives scent the air next to a superb variety of smoked meats: hams from Virginia, Vermont, and Parma; Spanish *chorizo*, French *saucisson*, German *wurst* and *Bundnerfleisch*; Italian salamis and *soppressata*.

A fresh-fish counter, prepared salads and entrees, and a meat counter flank the central aisle displays of preserves, coffees and teas, biscuits, herbs and spices, dried pastas and beans, and a fragrant bread counter with everything from *focaccio* to sourdough baguettes. Top-quality produce and a dairy case with such gourmet treats as crème fraîche round out the edible offerings. At the back of the store are cookbooks, quality cookware, dishes, and glassware. Although Dean & DeLuca prices are not low, the store is always thronged with foodies seeking a gourmet fix.

The Guggenheim Museum in Soho, 575 Broadway (at Prince Street), in a beautiful red-brick and cast-iron building, is an excellent example of the commercial/manufacturing loft architecture that gives Soho its unique character. Constructed in 1881 for John Jacob Astor III, the building was designed by Thomas Stent. The museum galleries are exceptionally spacious, occupying 8,000 square feet on the first floor and over 20,000 square feet on the second. The street-level museum shop carries books, posters, postcards, and art reproductions.

The museum's inaugural show, in June 1992, was *The Guggenheim Museum and the Art of This Century,* an overview of the development of the avant garde set against a backdrop of late 19th-century paintings. "Art of This Century" was the name of the art gallery opened in October 1942 by Peggy Guggenheim, whose private collection

The Guggenheim Museum in Soho, opening day, July 1, 1992

became the nucleus for the museum. Avant-garde architect Frederick Kieser designed her gallery with curving walls and wooden biomorphic furniture; it resembled a tunnel carved through a mountain.

Peggy Guggenheim gave one-man shows to Jackson Pollock, Hans Hofmann, Robert Motherwell, Mark Rothko, Jean Arp, Max Ernst (who was Guggenheim's husband at that time), and Alberto Giacometti long before they were established as modern masters. When her gallery opened, she was careful to wear one earring designed by Yves Tanguy and one by Alexander Calder, "in order to show no partiality between surrealist and abstract art." After the Second World War, Guggenheim closed her gallery and moved to Venice.

The New Museum of Contemporary Art, 583 Broadway (at Prince Street), which has no permanent collection, is a constantly evolving survey of new modern art. Almost without exception, all the shows focus on work produced since the gallery opened in 1973. The New Museum does not attract big names to its small exhibition space. Mixed-media artists like John Cage, Jeff Koons, Ed Ruscha, Keith Haring, and Glenn Branca have all been included in shows. Most of the exhibits are group shows, usually revolving around a particular theme.

The heart of Broadway's art gallery district is the block between Prince and East Houston Streets. In seven buildings there are a total of forty-five galleries, with fifteen in 560 Broadway alone.

At the southwest corner of Broadway and East Houston Street, sculptor Forrest Myers has transformed a blank brick wall into a sculpture/mural. He affixed forty-two turquoise aluminum bars to the sky-blue painted wall in a neat geometric pattern. The effect is particularly striking in early-morning and late-day sunlight, when the wall is further adorned by the long shadows cast by the jutting bars.

The Cable Building, 611 Broadway (at Houston Street), is on the site of St. Thomas Episcopal Church (1826), which was one of the first buildings in the New York Gothic revival style. In 1892, architect Stanford White erected the current building, an imposing ten-story structure, for the Broadway Cable Traction Company. The company's name is etched in stone on the building. On the building's street level at the corner of Mercer and Houston Streets is the Angelica Film Center, an alternative film theater with six screens and 1,146 seats.

It's interesting to note that Broadway, which in the 1850s was certainly the Eastern boundary of Greenwich Village, was actually the location where Bohemia began. **Pfaff's Beer Hall** at 653 Broadway, in the basement of one of the wings of the Broadway Central Hotel, has been identified by Dr. Jan Seidler Ramirez of the Museum of the City of New York as the birthplace of Bohemia. Charlie Pfaff's, a smoke-filled cave, earned notoriety for "its late hours, foreign fare, dim, smoky atmosphere and its free-thinking, sexually integrated clientele," according to Dr. Seidler Ramirez. Walt Whitman was acknowledged in his day as Pfaff's resident Bohemian bard, especially after the publication of *Leaves of Grass* in 1855.

For over 100 years, the Broadway Central Hotel stood at what is approximately 673 Broadway. The hotel opened on August 25, 1870, and on August 3, 1973 the entire central part of the hotel collapsed to the ground. With some interesting architectural manipulation, the building was rebuilt with a facade restored to look exactly like the old hotel. There is no longer an entrance on Broadway, but apartments are reached through a Bleecker Street lobby.

The Broadway Central lives in memory today largely because of what happened there. On January 6, 1872, Jim Fisk, president of the Erie Railroad, was shot by a former business associate in a quarrel over Josie Mansfield, the actress. The hotel survived the scandal to become, in the mid-1920s, a Kosher hotel, the City's premier location

Tower Records

for weddings, honeymoons, banquets, and bar mitzvahs. By the 1960s, it had become the most notorious welfare hotel in New York. After I took a photo that was published in the *Village Voice* of a female tenant with a twelve-inch butcher knife chasing a security guard, the politicians and the public took notice. The hotel was eventually cleaned up, but its poor maintenance led to its collapse.

At Broadway and East 4th Street looms **Tower Records**, which has fast become one of the major axes of Broadway in the Village. One of two stores of this retail

124

music outlet in New York, Tower, with its unbelievably varied and huge inventory, attracts music fans from all over the metropolitan area. Its four floors are an overwhelming experience for the music fan who can find nearly every recording available today, plus other music-related media like magazines and videotapes.

Because so many people jam the sidewalks around the store, impromptu flea markets have sprung up in the empty space right next to Tower, and street vendors now show their merchandise on the sidewalk from the store all the way south to East Houston Street and north to Astor Place, creating a pop culture street mall of sorts. Although it makes for a crowded sidewalk, these merchants guarantee that you can stay in vogue with four-dollar imitation designer sunglasses, "authentic" Rolex watches, and other ersatz fashions.

Directly behind Tower Records is Tower Video, 383 Lafayette Street (at East 4th Street), and above it **Tower Books**. The bookstore is particularly impressive, with good selections of books on New York, fine art, the performing arts, and a dizzying array of magazines, domestic and foreign, in addition to the expected bestsellers. The video outlet outdoes your local rental store by offering more foreign and off-beat titles, plus a full selection of films on laser disc.

Sandwiched between Broadway's cast-iron landmarks, the art galleries, and the fabric stores is the **New York University Tisch School of the Arts**, 721 Broadway (at Washington Place), which celebrated its twenty-fifth anniversary in 1990. The school is at the forefront of performing and visual arts education but its fame and glory centers on its famous faculty and alumni. Graduates include filmmakers Martin Scorcese, Oliver Stone, Susan Seidelman, Spike Lee, Joel Coen, Jim Jarmusch, Amy Heckerling, Joel Silver, Jane Rosenthal, and actor Alec Baldwin.

Educating artists to discover their own voices is the foundation of the school's success says David Oppenheim, the school's dean for over twenty years. Considering the school a "classic conservatory," the Tisch School is divided into the Institute of Performing Arts and the Institute of Film and Television. Within these two institutes, departments include cinema studies, interactive telecommunications, dramatic writing, musical theatre, photography, acting, dance, and design. Most programs are offered at the undergraduate and graduate levels.

Grace Episcopal Church

Once a marginal appendage of NYU, the Tisch School is now one of the University's most prestigious divisions. Fueled by the constant and recurring success of its students, the school has been the recipient of many large monetary gifts, the most notable, of course, from Laurence and Preston Robert Tisch of Loews Corporation and CBS, who pledged seven-and-a-half million dollars and enabled the school to move into its present home in a converted textile building on lower Broadway. Coincidentally, Oppenheim remembers that Larry Tisch told him that "this was the building where his father had worked making trousers." Tisch includes over a thousand undergraduate and graduate students, taught by over two hundred full- and part-time faculty.

Astor Place Hair Designers International, 2 Astor Place (at Broadway), is the classic barbershop with clients coming from all over the City, often to wait in line for their favorite barber. Every weekend the place is jammed with young and old customers spilling on to the sidewalk. Both men and women come for a "Mow-hawk," an "Elvis cut," a "buzz cut," and some even get it all cut off and walk out bald and proud. Astor Place gives good permanents and color rinses at unbeatable prices. The Macy's of the barber world, Astor Place can accommodate over fifty customers on three levels of hair-styling mayhem.

Grace Episcopal Church at Broadway and 10th Street is one of New York's most attractive landmarks. The church, built in 1846, was designed by Hendrick Brevoort's grandson, James Renwick, a twenty-three-year-old construction engineer who had never studied architecture. Entering a competition to produce an outstanding design for Grace Church, Renwick studied pictures of the great European cathedrals, incorporated their best features, and submitted a plan that won the contest and proved to be a revolutionary influence on American church architecture. His design was basically English Gothic in style with flamboyant touches. Renwick later designed St. Patrick's Cathedral and the Smithsonian Institution in Washington. In the meantime, he even acquired an architect's degree.

One of the more colorful episodes in the history of the church was the wedding on February 10, 1863 of P. T. Barnum's famed sideshow midgets, General Tom Thumb and Lavinia Warren Bumpus. Barnum planned the nuptials shrewdly foreseeing the promotional value of this calculated media event. Because a wedding at Grace Church was synonymous with wealth and social eminence, its aristocratic parishioners were enraged by the rector's edict that "little people have as much right as anybody else to get married in a big church." However, the church members were as curious as they were outraged, and 1,200 of them stormed the church, jostling each other vigorously, trampling the expensively upholstered pews in their attempt to get a better view of the ceremony, and in general presenting a marked contrast to the dignified behavior of the couple getting married.

The tract on which the church stands was once the property of Hendrick Brevoort, a monumentally stubborn old farmer who, as legend tells, single-handedly altered the map of Manhattan. According to the City Board of Commissioner's layout of the City streets, both 11th Street and Broadway were to cut through Brevoort's property. However, in 1847, Hendrick rejected the plan because it meant the destruction of his favorite elm tree. Until his death at ninety-four, Hendrick resisted the construction crews despite several city ordinances demanding him to yield. As a result of his defiance, Broadway today curves west, avoiding his property, and 11th Street stops on the west side of Broadway and resumes on the east side of Fourth Avenue.

Fred Bass, who runs the **Strand Book Store**, 828 Broadway at 12th Street, is one of the most knowledgeable book people in New York. Some believe that he is familiar with nearly every book in his store. The Strand is New York's largest used bookstore with two million books on eight miles of shelves and sells current review copies of books at 50 percent off retail price. The Strand also buys books, and is one of the most popular bookstores for bargain hunters, intellectuals, and those looking for out-of-print and rare collectors' volumes. The truly rare books are quietly housed next door to the main, bustling shop; ask at the sale's desk for directions.

Across the street from the Strand at 821 Broadway is **Forbidden Planet**, the world's largest science-fiction megastore that is the headquarters for sci-fi fans. Forbidden Planet is stocked with comics, T-shirts, toys, models, role-playing games like Dungeons and Dragons, posters, figures, and many other products related to space and the imagination. Considered a freak shop by the small-minded, Forbidden Planet was one of the first stores to realize that there was a billion-dollar industry lurking in the recesses of the dark, imaginative minds of Trekkies and other fantasy fans.

Union Square

Union Square achieved its identity as the center of American radical activity and as a forum for mass protest during the Civil War. The Square was also the location of meetings, reviews, and parades for departing Union troops. On September 21, 1882, 10,000 members of the Knights of Labor marched around Union Square, inspiring a national holiday, Labor Day. The Knights of Labor, started by Philadelphia tailors in 1869, was organized to include women, African-American workers, and even their employers. Only bankers, lawyers, gamblers, and stockholders were excluded. The Knights of Labor advocated an eight-hour day, abolition of child and convict labor, equal pay for equal work, and elimination of private banks. This idealistic labor organization aided various groups in strikes and boycotts.

Until the turn of the century, Union Square was the center of the city's musical, theatrical, and merchandising activity. After the First World War, Union Square began to assume its importance as an open-air soapbox for anarchists, socialists, and wobblies. On August 22, 1927, the night set for the execution in Boston of the anarchists Nicola Sacco and Bartolomeo Vanzetti, a shoemaker and a fish peddler, machine guns were mounted on the roof of Klein's department store to insure crowd control. On May 18, 1929, the Communist Party led one of the first "anti-Police brutality" demonstrations there. After the 1929 stock market crash, the Square became the gathering place for the jobless. The largest demonstration ever held in Union Square was on March 6, 1930 when more than 35,000 unemployed workers crowded in the park demanding jobs. When the demonstrators started to march to City Hall, the police broke up the protest parade, injuring hundreds of people.

Union Square as a cultural district had its beginnings in 1854 when the Academy of Music, 126 East 14th Street, opened as the home of grand opera. It is now the home of **The Palladium**, a major concert venue for pop and rock 'n' roll acts, a dancehall for celebrity parties, and home to the cable television program, *Club MTV*. In 1882, August Luchow founded his restaurant on 110 East 14th Street, a celebrated German beer-hall style restaurant, and it survived nearly one hundred years. Klein's on the Square, the last of the great bargain-basement department stores, closed soon after Luchow's. The streets took up

Jodie Foster, Martin Scorsese, and Robert De Niro shooting Taxi Driver *in a cafeteria at Third Avenue and East 13th Street, July 25, 1975*

130

the slack, with hawkers and pitchmen finding easy pickings among the poor and naive looking for bargains. The street and park are magnets for pretzel vendors, blind singers, legless beggars on roller-skate platforms, the homeless holding styrofoam coffee cups seeking quarters, and fly-by-night sharpies selling tape decks, radios, and camcorders of dubious value and origin. Buy cheap junk, get cheap junk.

In recent years, Union Square has achieved some respectability with the construction of the high-rise Zeckendorf Tower, which replaced Klein's on the Square. The park recently received a stunning renovation including trimmed hedges and trees that allow for prominent sightlines. The park's famous statues can be seen again: George Washington by Henry Kirke Brown erected in 1856 is the oldest statue in New York still in its original location. Going in a circle, there is the Marquis de Lafayette by Frederic August Bartholdi, done in 1876; Abraham Lincoln also by Brown, from 1869; and Mohandes K. Gandhi by K. B. Patel, sculpted in 1976.

Throughout the year there is a **Greenmarket**, a huge open fruit, vegetable, and flower market, that operates three times a week and is reminiscent of farmers' markets in Paris. There are fresh fish from Montauk, organically grown radishes the size of baseballs from New Jersey, and ten different kinds of New York State apples, trucked in by farmers from upstate.

Many artists once lived on Union Square and along 14th Street. It was virtually an extension of Greenwich Village. Andy Warhol's famous Factory was on Union Square, and it was the location where a crazed, former Warhol underground film actress tried to assassinate him on June 3, 1968. Such artists as Max Weber, Walt Kuhn, Reginald Marsh, Joseph Stella, Walter Pach, Raphael Soyer, Morris Kantor, and Arshile Gorky made their homes here. Marcel Duchamp, the French expatriate Dada artist, lived at 210 West 14th Street, and down the block at number 242, Franz Kline, a key figure in the New York School of painting, lived in the brownstone studio one flight above street level.

The only remaining activity from Union Square's past may be Julian's famous pool room and the Variety Arts Theatre around the corner on Third Avenue. **Julian's 14th Street Billiard Academy** has been a New York City institution since 1909. Originally housed downtown at Broadway and Worth Street, the present-day Julian's, a

Franz Kline in his studio on 14th Street, April 7, 1961

quintessential, classic pool hall at 138 East 14th Street between Third and Fourth Avenues, has carried on the billiards tradition here since 1933. Climbing a staircase to Julian's, you will instantly hear the clicks, knocks, crashes, and padded thumps of billiard balls and see the green felts and lively colored pool balls scattering and then disappearing on some thirty full-size tables. Where once business deals were closed at lunch while suited men waited for their tables at Luchow's, Julian's now caters to a younger, hipper crowd equally as serious about their game.

Frank Julian did not serve refreshments, nor did his son Roland who ran things after him, and today you still have to bring your own food and drinks. A popular spot for an inexpensive date, Julian's is crowded on most nights with young men and women enjoying a game of skill. While most of the patrons are casual sports, there are still some very serious games going on, so be courteous and remember that money may be on your neighbor's next shot. Rack 'em up!

Around the corner, the **Variety Arts Theatre**, 110 Third Avenue, came into existence in 1914 as the Variety Photo Plays Theatre, and

The Variety Arts Theatre in its former life, December 16, 1965

was open until the 1980s with its sandwichboard lobby cards advertising western films. Here was the place to see triple features, with numerous cartoons and coming attractions. It was one of the first nickelodeons specifically built to feature "photo plays," two-reelers usually fifteen or twenty minutes long. In recent years, the theatre switched to raunchy and naughty films, was featured in a Madonna video, and finally closed, to be born again in the early 1990s as a legit, off-Broadway theatre. The Variety lives on!

Astor Place/Cooper Square

Astor Place is home to Bernard Rosenthal's 1967 cube sculpture "Alamo," which stands upright on a pedestrian island in the middle of Astor Place. Astor Place was named for the American fur trader and real-estate tycoon John Jacob Astor. His money financed the Astor Library at 425 Lafayette Street, which was the country's first public library. Theoretically, Astor set his library up for the poor, but, since the hours were only from ten to four, most workers could not make use of it. Furthermore, books could not be taken from the reading room, and pen and ink could not be used in taking notes. The merger of the Astor Library with the Tilden Trust and the Lenox Library formed the New York Public Library, which moved to its present Bryant Park location (Fifth Avenue and 42nd Street) in 1911. The Lafayette Street building was occupied by the Hebrew Immigrant Aid Society, and, since its purchase by Joseph Papp in 1965, has been the home of the New York Shakespeare Festival.

Astor Place was the site of the luxurious Astor Place Opera House that, on May 10, 1819, was the scene of the worst riot in the history of the theatre, accounting for thirty-one deaths and 150 casualties. In the light of the next day, the sight of the dead and dying shocked a city already torn by issues of class and wealth: an aristocracy sympathetic to all things English; a poor, uneducated underclass contemptuous of the rich and passionate about all things American.

This was the tragic culmination of a feud between two Shakespearean actors, American matinee idol Edwin Forrest and William Charles Macready, the English tragedian, who were both playing in competing productions of *Macbeth*. At the Opera House, Macready's appearance was greeted from the audience with rotten eggs, copper pennies, apples, potatoes, lemons, and assorted articles that splashed the actor's costume. The theatre was attacked by the mob inflamed by the abuse by English audiences of their hero Forrest. A crowd of 10,000 milled out of control outside the theatre and order wasn't restored until mounted police fired small arms and artillery into the mob. The opera house was left in shambles and demolished shortly after.

The **Joseph Papp Public Theatre**, 425 Lafayette (at Astor Place), is the home of the New York Shakespeare Festival, founded by Brooklyn-born Joseph Papp, one of the most influential producers in the history of the American theatre. In 1954, Papp started The Shakespeare Workshop in a church basement on the Lower East Side. In 1962, the Free Shakespeare Summer Festival became part of the Central Park landscape at the Delacorte Theatre. Papp saved the Astor Library from demolition, named it the Public Theatre, and had the building declared a landmark.

Joseph Papp (Sylvia Miles in background), May 21, 1973

In 1967, Joe Papp opened his new theatre with Jerome Ragni's and Galt MacDermott's production of *Hair,* which later was a huge success on Broadway. He championed the work of many contemporary playwrights, including David Rabe, Ed Bullins, Caryl Churchill, David Hare, David Henry Hwang, Wallace Shawn, Vaclav Havel, Miguel Pinero, Ntozake Shange, David Mamet, Tina Howe, and John

Guare. He helped build the careers of many actors, among them James Earl Jones, Meryl Streep, Raul Julia, and Kevin Kline. Papp, who produced over 400 plays and musicals, exercised a profound influence in bringing to the attention of the public the work of many important African-American, Hispanic, and Asian-American play-wrights and actors. Papp prided himself on being an outsider and a radical. When Miguel Pinero, an exconvict who wrote *Short Eyes,* an explosive look inside prisons, was arrested, Papp went to the police station to bail him out. Papp fought bureaucracy, unions, founda-tions, audiences, critics, and the City of New York.

Known all over the world, the Festival encompasses the Public Theatre with five stages and a cinema under one roof. Festival productions have collectively won twenty-eight Tony Awards, ninety-six OBIEs, twenty-nine Drama Desk Awards, six New York Drama Critics' Awards, and three Pulitzer Prizes. Seventeen productions have been transferred to the Broadway stage including *A Chorus Line,* the longest running show in the history of Broadway. Its success helped bankroll many of Papp's other projects. Other productions include Larry Kramer's *The Normal Heart,* the first major play about AIDS, which was one of the longest running plays in the Festival's history. Since it opened in 1985, it has had more than 600 productions worldwide.

In 1987, the New York Shakespeare Festival embarked on a marathon of presenting Shakespeare's entire thirty-six works featuring the foremost American theatrical and film actors. In 1990 Joe Papp named JoAnne Akalaitis, a founding member of the experimental troupe Mabou Mines, as his successor as Artistic Director of the New York Shakespeare Festival. He died of cancer in 1991. In 1992, the Public Theatre was renamed the Joseph Papp Public Theatre in his honor.

Colonnade Row, at 428 Lafayette Street across from the Public Theatre, is an elegant survival of the once-exclusive La Grange Terrace row of nine town houses. About one-half of the row remains, the other half having been converted into a factory building. In a pattern familiar to European cities, the entire group of houses was banded as one building in order to achieve a greater unity in design. When construction was completed on April 18, 1831, La Grange Terrace was considered the finest row of private dwellings in the City.

Washington Irving (aka Diedrich Knickerbocker) lived in Colon-nade row in 1836. He was the author of the 1821 *A History of*

New-York, from the beginning of the World to the end of the Dutch Dynasty; Containing, among many surprising and curious matters,

The Unutterable Ponderings of Walter The Doubter, The Disastrous Projects of William The Testy, and The Chivalric Achievements of Peter The Headstrong, The Three Dutch Governors of New-Amsterdam; Being the only authentic history of the times that ever hath been published, surely one of the longest titles ever appended to a literary work, and the famous *The Sketch Book,* which includes the story of Rip Van Winkle.

Fourth Avenue bookshops, 1950s

The Fourth Avenue bookstores that stretched from Astor Place to 14th Street have completely disappeared, with the lone exception of **Pageant Books,** 109 East 9th Street near Fourth Avenue. The distinguished row of secondhand book dealers was known throughout the world for their antiquarian books on every subject under the sun. Pageant Books and the Strand on Broadway are the only places now where one might find the classic eleventh edition of the *Encyclopedia Britannica,* first volumes of Horatio Alger's works, or Isaac Newton Phelps Stokes's six-volume *Iconography of Manhattan Island.* Pageant Books also carries the largest collection of antique maps and prints available in New York.

Cooper Union, at the crossroads of Third Avenue, 7th Street, and Cooper Square, is named after a remarkable American engineer and philanthropist, Peter Cooper. The son of an indigent country store-keeper, Cooper made a fortune in the iron industry and was president of the firm that laid the first cable across the Atlantic. Cooper was also a millionaire glue manufacturer and builder of the first American-made locomotive, The Tom Thumb.

With his millions, Cooper founded Cooper Union on February 17, 1857 as a free, coeducational institute of science and art open without racial or religious restriction to all who could pass its entrance examinations. The concept was a startling one for his day, and was the realization of a youthful dream of the founder, a millionaire who had

Cooper Union

not been able to afford even a high school education. Through the years the school has helped thousands of needy students to gain an education in engineering and art.

Cooper incorporated the latest developments in architectural technology in the construction of the school's building. To support the flooring, he used rolled, wrought iron beams arranged in a light grid, and by replacing heavy stone arches with thinner piers, he increased the usable space.

Cooper Union forum was, and still is, the meeting hall of reformers gathering their forces against corrupt City administrations. Henry Ward Beecher, William Cullen Bryant, William Lloyd Garrison, and others thundered there against slavery and in defense of the Union. Abraham Lincoln, on February 27, 1860, made the speech that is credited with winning him the nomination for the presidency.

Below the building, in triangle shaped Cooper Square, a statue of Peter Cooper executed by Cooper Union graduate Augustus Saint-Gaudens gazes down the Bowery.

Partisan Review was founded in 1934 as a forum for the discussion of Marxist-Leninist doctrine as it applied to art and

139

literature. Besides its political mission, the magazine was devoted to publishing avant-garde writers and to introducing new European authors to an American audience. *Partisan Review* printed Saul Bellow's first work and part of James T. Farrell's novel *Studs Lonigan*. In 1940, the magazine was edited out of Dwight MacDonald's apartment at 117 East 10th Street. The following year, it moved into 45 Astor Place, which until 1956 was the site of Bible House, but now is part of Cooper Union Engineering School. The editors were Philip Rahv, William Phillips, and Dwight MacDonald.

The *Review*'s radical politics were sorely tested by America's involvement in World War II. As described in John Tebbel's *The Magazine in America, "Partisan Review* had seen the conflict originally as an imperialistic event, but then Phillips changed his mind and supported American involvement. He was followed a little later by Rahv. MacDonald remained the holdout, and since he was the odd man out, making the editorial situation impossible, he was maneuvered off the magazine by the other two editors." Delmore Schwartz succeeded him. MacDonald then started *Politics,* which was published from 1944 to 1949 in the same building as *Partisan Review* at 45 Astor Place. The magazine still exists and is published in Boston.

The *Village Voice* newspaper, 36 Cooper Square (at 7th Street), began October 26, 1955 with psychologist Edwin Fancher as publisher and philosopher Daniel Wolf as editor. Norman Mailer, an original investor, wrote "Quickly, A Column for Slow Readers." The theatre editor, Jerry Tallmer, started the off-Broadway Theatre Awards (OBIEs). Poetry editor Harvey Shapiro sold advertising, John Wilcock was news editor, and poet Frank O'Hara was art critic in the very first issue. "Sick, Sick, Sick," the unusual title of Jules Feiffer's original cartoon panel, first appeared in the *Village Voice*. Contributors in the first issues included photographer Berenice Abbott, writers Vance Bourjaily, Michael Harrington, and Gerald Walker, cultural critic Casper H. Citron, arts columnist Gilbert Seldes, opera critic Leighton Kerner, jazz critic and social commentator Nat Hentoff, and a "Night People" column by the famous radio monologist Jean Shephard. Dan List, auto buff, delivered the papers to the newsstands. Mona Lurie, the unsung heroine of the *Voice*'s original one-person staff when the paper was published at 22 Greenwich Avenue, is still with the paper.

In many ways the *Village Voice* is the direct descendant of the first Bohemian weekly that was founded in October 1858 by Henry

Norman Mailer and editor Daniel Wolf in the Sheridan Square office of the Village Voice, *April 14, 1969*

Clapp, a journalist and theatre critic, called *The Saturday Press*. Everybody active in contemporary letters seemed to contribute even though, like the *Village Voice,* the pay was irregular, small, and often nothing. *The Saturday Press* began its career by spreading the praise of Walt Whitman and ended by introducing Mark Twain and his "Jumping Frog" to the Atlantic Coast, launching his nationwide fame. The financial nightmares of Henry Clapp kept him awake at night. Albert Parry points out in *Garrets and Pretenders* that "when the current backer had exhausted his patience and money, Henry would look for a new angle and on finding one would proceed to divide the fresh blood, as he called the new money, among his struggling friends. When the funds again came to an end, Clapp would barricade the editorial doors against the indignant creditors."

The *Village Voice* is now quite successful, a continuously entertaining and controversial forum for its reporters and columnists who take advantage of the opportunity the paper provides them to sound off on a wide variety of topics from politics to art to music to theatre to film to lesbian and gay rights. Even its curious classified ads have achieved fame of sorts. In 1959, I was selling ad space for the *Voice*

141

McSorley's Old Ale House

and, as a lark, ran a small, two-line notice for a "Rent-a-Beatnik" service. The resulting publicity led to interviews on nationwide TV, great publicity for the *Voice,* and several successful Beatnik parties. Even *Mad* magazine got into the act, parodying my ad in their "Rent-a-Square" notice.

The current publisher, David Schneiderman, and editor, Jonathan Z. Larsen, have managed to lead the *Voice* into the 1990s with determination to maintain its reputation as a great writer's paper and a showcase for exceptional photography. As the *Village Voice* heads into its fourth decade, it still divides its readers into two camps: those who hate the paper and those who love it.

About a block away from the *Village Voice* building at 15 East 7th Street is the famous **McSorley's Old Ale House,** probably the oldest saloon in America. Established in 1854, it has so far survived everything from revolutions to real-estate agents. Still occupying its original home, McSorley's features a potbelly stove, old gas lamps, and a carved mahogany bar. The pressed tin walls are covered with ephemera collected by John McSorley before his death in 1910, including a rare poster offering a reward for Abraham Lincoln's assassin. McSorley's was off-limits to female customers until 1971, when, under court order, women were admitted.

Drinking and relaxing at McSorley's have not changed much over the years, and on weekends the place is jammed. Don't go for a cocktail though because all that is served is ale, dark or light, served in rounds, which simply means two mugs at a time. For those not drinking ale, you can order cola or leave!

The Bowery

Sammy's Bowery Follies; The Knitting Factory; The Original Yonah Schimmel Knishery; Russ & Daughters Appetizing Store; Ben's Cheese Shop; Moishe's Homemade Kosher Bakery; Katz's Delicatessen; Keith Haring Pop Shop; Old St. Patrick's Cathedral and Cemetery; Bayard-Condict Building; CBGB&OMFUG; Amato Opera Theatre; Bond Street Savings Bank/Bouwerie Lane Theatre; Firehouse Engine Company 33; Old Merchant's House

During the '50s, the search for low-cost rentals brought writers and artists into the Bowery in increasing numbers. Previously its sidewalks were practically the exclusive domain of drunks, panhandlers, derelicts, and vagrants. The street is still lined with restaurant supply stores, chair and barstool dealers, flophouses, saloons, secondhand clothing stores, and all-night missions. Overhead elevated trains once rumbled and creaked, either blotting out the sun or causing it to cast ominous shadows on the street below. The tracks were torn down in 1955, but bright sunlight, young Villagers, and remodeled storefronts have not yet completely altered the street's identity. At Cooper Square the Bowery becomes Third Avenue.

The Bowery lost what little glitter it had when **Sammy's Bowery Follies** at 267 Bowery closed in 1970. The building is now Attias, a manufacturer of pizza ovens. The nationally known gay-nineties saloon, where drifters, the rich, and the forgotten mingled for nearly four decades in rowdy laughter and melancholy song disappeared forever. Its business was booming during World War II, but inflation and television closed it down.

The Knitting Factory, 47 East Houston Street (at Mulberry Street), directed by Michael Dorf and Bob Appel, is located in what once must have been a fancy town house 100 years ago. The front now looks like a dizzying billboard collage with hundreds of posters pasted one on top of another. Just down the block is Ballato's famous Italian restaurant at 55 East Houston Street.

Open every night, the Knitting Factory is a club where cutting-edge performance art—spoken word, dance, video, acoustic solo and duo lineups, avant-garde and experimental jazz, and progressive rock—fills the narrow space with customers who are jammed together at tiny triangular-shaped tables. The lineup of musicians and composers includes Cecil Taylor, John Zorn, Elliott Sharp, Robin Holcomb, Odean Pope, Butch Morris, Wayne Horovitz, Bobby Previte, Milt Hinton, and Geri Allen.

Although many of the old-time Jewish storekeepers have left the area east of Third Avenue, a few hardy survivors of the original community remain. **The Original Yonah Schimmel Knishery**, 137 East Houston Street (at Forsyth Street), is the Jewish bakery that claims to have invented the knish. This Jewish delicacy is available here in many varieties, including the ever-popular potato and, my personal favorite, the kasha knish. They also feature many other old-world delicacies, including borscht, liver puffs, potato latkes, and blueberry, cherry-cheese, and apple strudel. The outside of the store may look a little decrepit, but the interior has the same Old World atmosphere it had when it first opened in 1910. There are nine small tables available for customers, plus everything is available for take out.

For New Yorkers of Eastern European descent, a trio of adjoining stores along Houston Street offers a culinary mecca. The nostalgic aromas wafted about in **Russ & Daughters Appetizing Store**, 179 East Houston Street (at Orchard Street), are mouthwatering reminders of Mama's Sunday-morning spreads. It's all here: fresh homemade cream cheeses (plain, chive, or vegetable); gleaming smoked fish (whitefish, sturgeon, sable, and five kinds of lox); pickled herring fillets (matjes, herring in cream or wine sauce, rollmops); prepared salads; rock candy, halvah, and other sweets; and a selection of coffees, teas, and fancy groceries for an extra gourmet touch. Open barrels of dill pickles and pickled tomatoes, olives, and red peppers spice the fragrant air.

Head next door to **Ben's Cheese Shop,** 181 East Houston Street, for a rare (and low cholesterol/low calorie) treat: homemade farmer cheese. It's fresh or baked, and comes in an amazing variety of sweet or savory flavors: blueberry, strawberry, peach, chive, vegetable, or onion. You'll find good buys as well in other cheeses (Swiss, Brie, and cheddar) at Ben's.

Stop into the adjoining **Moishe's Homemade Kosher Bakery,** 181 East Houston Street (at Orchard Street), to pick up fresh bagels and bialys to complete this quintessentially New York ethnic meal. Also featured here are the crusty sour rye and corn breads, challah (egg-bread twist), and pumpernickel that are the staples of an Eastern European diet. Moishe's also purveys such oldtime favorites as babka and other cinnamon-scented coffee cakes, poppyseed strudel, and chocolate seven-layer cake.

Katz's Delicatessen, 205 East Houston Street (at Ludlow Street), deserves every award displayed in its window. The menu offers a complete rundown of kosher-style deli, with pastrami, corned beef, tongue, salami, franks, and such tasty side dishes as knishes, sauerkraut, baked beans, and french fries. Keeping up with the times, Katz's has a fax machine (212-674-3270) to serve your lunch or dinner needs. This 100-year-old New York institution achieved worldwide recognition from its patriotic World War II slogan "Send a salami to your boy in the Army." It also achieved cinematic recognition in a hilarious scene in *When Harry Met Sally,* when Meg Ryan, seated at a table in the deli, forthrightly simulated the groaning ecstasy of an orgasm as Billy Crystal, in growing horror, sat across the table from her.

The Keith Haring Pop Shop

The **Keith Haring Pop Shop**, 292 Lafayette Street (at East Houston Street), is virtually a shrine to this famous graffiti artist who died of AIDS in 1990. The unique store is decorated from floor to ceiling with Haring's work, creating a total environment. Haring's graphic talents made him one of the stars of the 1980s art scene. During his brief but meteoric career, Haring invented a cartoonish universe inhabited by crawling children, barking dogs, and dancing figures, all set in motion by heavy black lines. His best-known images include the "Radiant Child," a crawling infant surrounded by rays of light, and the "Barking Dog," an alligator-like creature stylized like Egyptian hieroglyphics. Not only were Haring's images widely admired, the morality tales they portrayed were easy to understand. As his art became better-known, Haring's prices skyrocketed to as much as $350,000. He was also known for his huge mural of the Ten Commandments for the Contemporary Art Museum in Bordeaux, France, and a 3,000-foot painting of a chain of red-and-black figures that was on the Berlin Wall. Haring opened The Pop Shop in 1986; a commercial venture, it sells T-shirts, toys, and posters for anti-apartheid and AIDS-related causes.

Old St. Patrick's Cathedral and Cemetery, 233 Mott Street (at Prince Street), is tucked away on a quiet corner just a few steps from the Bowery. The redbrick church was built in 1809 and is the predecessor of the much grander and more famous cathedral on Fifth Avenue at 51st Street. Mother Elizabeth Seton opened the first Catholic orphanage at Old St. Patrick's. She founded New York's first charitable organization, the Society for Relief of Poor Widows with Small Children, as well as the Sisters of Mercy, a teaching order of nuns. She has been canonized and is the first American-born saint.

The church still has an active local parish and school, and is seeking to claim another candidate for sainthood: Pierre Toussaint. He was born into slavery in Haiti in 1766, and was brought to New York City in 1787 with his owner. The owner returned to Haiti, leaving his family in dire straits. Toussaint, who was a hairdresser, supported the family from his earnings. He also raised money to help neglected children and nursed victims of a yellow fever epidemic. Toussaint was the only black buried in Old St. Patrick's Church Cemetery. As one of the initial steps toward possible canonization, his remains were exhumed in 1991.

Built in 1897, the **Bayard-Condict Building**, 65 Bleecker Street (at Lafayette Street), is the only building in New York City designed by Louis H. Sullivan, the first American to work in a nonhistoric, modern architectural style. The first modern skyscraper in New York, its vertical design is an expression of Sullivan's theory of the skyscraper as a "proud and soaring thing." It is distinguished by its terra-cotta facade ornamented with leafy forms.

CBGB&OMFUG, 315 Bowery (at Bleecker Street), is an acronym for Country, Blue Grass, Blues and Other Music for Uplifting Gourmandizers. Club owner Hilly Kristal, a punk-rock father-figure and cultivator of the Hell's Angels look, opened CBGB in March 1974 with Richard Hell, bass player for the group Television, the first psychosexual rock group. Previously, he had operated a bar called Kristal's at the same location that catered to a motorcycle-and-leather crowd. That performance was followed by The Ramones, Patti Smith, James Chance, Debbie Harry of Blondie, Stiv Bators, The Dead Boys, David Byrne of Talking Heads, The Butthole Surfers, and Missing Foundation—the self-styled anarchist East Village rock group that in one performance doused their drums with kerosene, lit a match, and set the club on fire. On another memorable evening, Wendy W. Williams of the Plasmatics created a new style when she brought a chain saw on stage and cut a guitar in half directly into the sound system to ensure that the buzz would be loud enough to be heard all over the room.

At CBGB, hard-core rock groups created another new art form by diving off the stage into the audience to force their apathetic fans out of their traditional passivity as they stood snapping their fingers and staring at the performers. Other groups have spat at, poured beer on, cursed, thrown up on, stomped on, and generally humiliated their fans, who remarkably seem to enjoy the verbal and physical abuse. After they've had enough of this, the audience checks out the CBGB art gallery or CBGB pizza parlor next door that features great pizza, a pool table, and a full service bar.

The **Amato Opera Theatre**, 319 Bowery (at Bleecker Street), was founded in 1948 as a nonprofit organization under the direction of Anthony Amato. The opera theatre provides a testing ground for young singers seeking training and experience in opera. "Opera-in-Brief," performed in schools, parks, and community centers, provides young people with a pleasurable entry into, and understanding of, the wonderful world of opera. The Amato Opera has presented thousands

148

Frank's Museum (l to r: Steve Levant, Frank Ruscitti, Jo Boy, Sal Cataldi) perform at CBGB&OMFUG, February 29, 1992

of performances of the world's greatest repertoire operas, plus such rarely performed works as Guiseppe Verdi's *I Due Foscari,* Umberto Giordano's *La cena delle beffe,* Luigi Ricci's *Crispino e la comare,* and American premieres of Verdi's *Oberto, Alzira, Aroldo, Un Giorno di Regno,* and *La Battaglia di Legnano,* Antonio Carlos Gomes's *Salvator Rosa* and *Lo Schiavo,* and Arrigo Boito's *Nerone.*

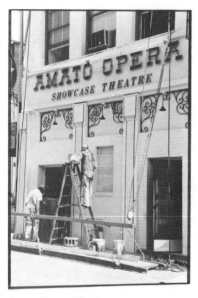

Amato Opera Theatre

The **Bond Street Savings Bank,** 330 Bowery (at Bond Street), is an especially interesting cast-iron building, designed by Henry Engelbert in the elaborate style of the French Second Empire. The architect was faced with the problem of creating an impressive bank building with only a twenty-five foot facade on the more important of the two thoroughfares. He solved this problem by designing an elaborate entrance on the Bowery and giving the Bond Street side a facade of considerable elegance. The wealth of ornamental detail makes this building an unusually fine example of cast-iron construction. Upon completion in 1874, it was known as the Bond Street Bank, and later became the German Exchange Bank, then a loft building. In 1963, it took on an entirely different character as the home of the **Bouwerie Lane Theater,** home of the Jean Cocteau Repertory company. These varied uses demonstrate how a century-old building can meet changing needs without compromising its architectural integrity.

The **Firehouse Engine Company 33,** 44 Great Jones Street (at the Bowery), was completed in 1898 by architects W. B. Chambers and Brooklyn-born Ernest Flagg, who also designed New York's Singer Building and St. Luke's Hospital, and the Corcoran Gallery in Washington. This late 19th-century firehouse is a striking example of Beaux Arts style architecture. A daring design in its day, the impressive facade contains a number of elements that are strongly influenced by the French Louis XV style. For a utilitarian building, its design has

150

a flamboyance that seems particularly appropriate to the thrilling, but hazardous, profession its occupants follow. The four-story building's facade features an immense arch that swoops up three stories high to an elegantly carved keystone above an ornate cartouche.

New York City's Fire Department had its origins in the Dutch settlement of New Amsterdam, when the first fire ordinance was adopted by the settlers in 1648 under the administration of Governor Stuyvesant. The first paid firefighting company went into service on July 31, 1865. From this modest beginning, the department has grown to more than 10,500 firefighters.

The street where the **Old Merchant's House**, 29 East 4th Street (at the Bowery), stands was once very fashionable, lined with beautiful town houses. Now there are trucking garages, factories, rundown lofts, and an occasional rooming house on the block. It is one of the finest examples of classic Greek Revival architecture in the city. The only other group of such town houses remaining intact stands along Washington Square North. The Old Merchant's House is distinguished from the Washington Square buildings by its preservation of the original furnishings and interiors, left exactly as they were in 1835, when Seabury Tredwell, a merchant and hardware importer, moved into the house, which had been built five years earlier by Joseph Brewster.

When Gertrude Tredwell, Seabury's last child, died in 1933, the Tredwell house and its contents were scheduled for public auction to satisfy debts and the mortgage. George Chapman, a distant relative, created the Historic Landmark Society to take over the house. His purpose was to preserve it as a public museum displaying the family's entire belongings—paintings, furniture, china, lamps, books, even the framed diplomas from the fashionable girls' schools of the time.

In the house are trunks full of clothes, gowns, gloves, hats,

The Old Merchant's House

151

Chantilly lace, paisley shawls, satin dancing slippers, even an exquisitely embroidered christening bonnet. On the main floor is a huge double drawing room, cut in half by Corinthian columns and a sliding double door. On the second floor is a secret trapdoor that once led to an underground tunnel said to lead as far as the East River. The tunnel, one of a number in old Village homes, originally was designed supposedly as a means of escape in case the British invaded New York again. Such trapdoors were later utilized to help slaves escaping to Canada via the Underground Railway. The Old Merchant's House is open to the public for guided tours at various hours during the week.

East Village/St. Marks Place

Beats/Hippies/Yippies; Artists and Poets; St. Marks Place; St. Marks Bookstore; The Dom; Peace Eye Book Store; Performance Space 122; Mabou Mines; Theatre for the New City; Café Sin-é; Tompkins Square Park; First Houses; The Living Theatre; Nuyorican Poets Café

The East Village is located between 14th and East Houston Streets, and from Third Avenue to Avenue C. It has always contained a diverse population. At the turn of the century, it was predominantly a German community. After World War I, the Germans moved uptown. Within a few years, Poles, Ukrainians, Greeks, Russians, Jews, and Italians moved in, and Puerto Ricans and African-Americans came later. Beginning in the 1950s, artists, students, Hippies, Beatniks, and still later Yuppies—the young upwardly mobile professionals—migrated from Greenwich Village.

Some of the new renegades are from comfortable middle class suburban homes who have swarmed to the East Village in search of a simpler way of life, and some secretly live off trust funds. With long hair in ponytails, tiny earrings, colorful, torn jackets and blue jeans, they are a distinctive part of the neighborhood. A walk on the wild side of the East Village leaves the impression that absolutely nothing has changed since the days of anarchy and war and draft protests.

The East Village is still a cross-section of each generation past, from authentic old fashioned Bohemians and Beatniks, fistflying

Anarchists, scruffy radicals, and the counterculture Yippies (the Youth International Party founded by the late Abbie Hoffman, radical-turned-stockbroker Jerry Rubin, and "Yippie Conspirator" and editor of *The Realist,* Paul Krassner). In recent years, the protest movement focused on the senseless shutting down of Tompkins Square Park and the total destruction, with City Hall approval, of the park's bandshell. The objective was to get rid of "undesirables" (i.e., the homeless) who used the bandshell for shelter.

St. Marks Place doorway

Gentrification, which started two decades ago, did not seem to progress too far, due mostly to neighborhood opposition. Some real-estate sharpies took over a few 19th-century old-law tenements on bombed out streets, co-oped the apartments, sold two-room, sixth-floor walkups for astronomical prices, and left town. Still, in spite of these changes, the East Village remains a major center for experimental theatre, performance art, avant-garde poetry, and progressive music.

The first group to move from Greenwich Village to the East Village across the old boundary of Broadway were the painters and sculptors who took studios and lofts there in the late 1940s. Willem de Kooning moved into 88 East 10th Street; Milton Resnick was in the same building. Paul Georges was at 231 East 11th Street; Joan Mitchell at 60 St. Marks Place; William Littlefield lived in 537 East 13th Street, a few buildings down from number 210 where Emma Goldman, the founding mother of American Feminism, Socialism, and other radical causes, lived in 1903; Angelo Ippolito was in 315 East 10th Street; Wilfred Zogbaum at number 62; and Norman Bluhm lived at 68 East 12th Street. The renowned art critic Harold Rosenberg, who did much to champion the new art, lived at 117 East 10th Street.

Writers and poets also migrated to the East Village. In 1951, Norman Mailer took a fifth-floor tenement railroad flat at 41 First

154

Avenue near 2nd Street, next door to Daniel Wolf, who later became editor of the *Village Voice*. (I inherited Mailer's flat some years later and can testify that it was a dump!) In that same year, Allen Ginsberg and Peter Orlovsky moved into 206 East 7th Street and have remained in the East Village ever since. Ginsberg entertained William Burroughs, Jack Kerouac, Gregory Corso, and Herbert Huncke in this apartment at one time or another.

In 1953, W. H. Auden rented a parlor floor in a brownstone at 77 St. Marks Place, now a shrine of sorts. Frank O'Hara, the famous Harvard poet and art critic, lived from 1959 until 1964 at 441 East 9th Street along with a million-dollars worth of art by Willem de Kooning, Helen Frankenthaler, Robert Motherwell, Franz Kline, and Joan Mitchell. O'Hara—who was also a curator at the Museum of Modern Art, collector, author, and playwright—was run over by a beach taxi on Fire Island on July 25, 1966.

The gateway to the East Village is St. Marks Place. Left over from the days the Germans occupied the East Village is the beautifully preserved *Deutsch Americanische Schutzen Geselischaft,* or The German American Shooting Club, building located at 12 St. Marks Place. This organization built the ornate structure in 1888. The very hip, radical, well-informed St. Marks Bookshop now occupies the street level of this building.

St. Marks Place is like somebody's living room with an ongoing party. It's filled with noise and with street peddlers selling everything from exotic incense to used books to used clothing to the contents of someone's apartment, re-

Andy Warhol tries on an antique bandsman's uniform in a used clothing store on St. Marks Place, December 1966

cently looted, and spread out all along the curbside. St. Marks Place is a jumble of cubbyhole restaurants, fashionable boutiques, neighborhood saloons, record shops, and souvenir shops with "Godfather" printed license plates and Elvis T-Shirts.

At the corner of Second Avenue and St. Marks Place is the landmark newsstand Gem Spa, a neighborhood institution. The Dom, (Polski Dom Harodowy), now a nondescript community center at 23 St. Marks Place, was originally a huge dancehall and bar. Then the owners leased it to Jackie Cassen, an artist who had collaborated with LSD-guru Timothy Leary on theatrical "Psychedelic Celebrations." In April 1966, Andy Warhol and Paul Morrisey sublet the space for a month to present The Exploding Plastic Inevitable, a live performance of Andy Warhol films—*Vinyl, Sleep, Eat, Kiss,* and *Empire*—with live music performed by the Velvet Underground (Lou Reed, John Cale, Maureen Tucker, Sterling Morrison), along with the model-turned-singer Nico and Gerard Malanga dancing. David Bourdon in his definitive Warhol biography describes it this way:

> For the entire month, the Dom was the hip home for Warhol's psychedelic extravaganza. Andy himself, attired in black leather jacket, polo shirt and black chinos seldom ventured from his station on the balcony . . . The movies were usually projected three at a time onto the rear of the stage and the flanking walls, beaming huge close-ups of Mario Montez licking a banana, Robert Indiana nibbling a mushroom, and [Gerard] Malanga (in *Vinyl*) getting his T-shirt ripped off his torso. Meanwhile, the spotlights aimed at revolving mirrored balls transformed the ceiling and upper walls of the dark cavernous hall into a crazy night sky with thousands of flurrying stars. The Plastic Inevitable demonstrated Warhol's facility in conjuring a make-believe realm that encouraged people to see themselves as they wanted to be.

When the Warhol show closed, The Electric Circus, a disco, took over The Dom for a brief period.

Fans of the '60s art-rock, pornographic, stick-it-in-your-face band the Fugs will want to pay homage at the site of the **Peace Eye Book Store**, 383 East 10th Street (at Avenue C). Owned and operated by chief Fug Ed Sanders, the bookstore operated out of a storefront that had once been home to a kosher chicken dealer; the original Hebrew sign remained on the window. The bookstore was open only at night. In Sanders' words, it was the "Lower East Side's most sinister book shop . . . operated as a book scene, freak center, and scrounge

The opening of Andy Warhol's Exploding Plastic Inevitable at the Dom,
April 1, 1966

lounge." Sanders also published the controversial journal, *Fuck You: A Magazine of the Arts,* that was so obscene it could neither be sent through the mail nor sold; copies could only be given away to the sympathetic literati. The magazine featured poetry and diatribes by Sanders, Tuli Kupferberg (also a Fug), LeRoi Jones (aka Amiri Baraka), and even W. H. Auden. The Fugs were the original punk-rock band, spitting on the conventions of both folk-protest music and mainstream, commercial rock 'n' roll.

Performance Space 122, 150 First Avenue (at 9th Street), is an old public-school building converted into a not-for-profit arts center, where you can see dance, music, theatre, media, and visual artists in action. The space holds performance series in its two theaters as well as classes and workshops. Featured presentations include Avant-Garde-Arama, New Stuff, The Hearings, Reel Time, La Misma Onda, Hothouse, and P.S. 122 Field Trips. Performance Space 122 was founded by Tim Miller, Charles Moulton, and Charles Dennis, and is run by Mark Russell and Robin Schatell.

If there is an avant garde left in New York or a New Bohemia, or an echo of the old Greenwich Village, then it would be right here at P.S. 122 where downtown performance art is king. The ongoing luminaries and groups who have performed there reads like a *Who's Who* of performance art: Eric Bogosian, Spalding Gray, Karen Finley, Penny Arcade, Quentin Crisp, Bill Irwin, Meredith Monk, Peter Sellars, Bebe Miller, Ann Carlson, Yoshiko Chuma, Michael Smith and Doug Skinner, Jennifer Muller, Jane Comfort, Ishmael Houston-Jones, Afro-Ditee, Paul Zaloom, Dancenoise, the Blue Man Group, and Reno.

Mabou Mines has its headquarters in P.S. 122 and performs in art galleries, museums, and theatres, but does not maintain a permanent performance space. Mabou Mines was "born" in 1970

Karen Finley on Avenue B, April 27, 1990

while JoAnne Akalaitis, Lee Breuer, Philip Glass, Ruth Maleczech, and David Warrilow rehearsed *The Red Horse Animation* in a college in Nova Scotia near a defunct mining village named Mabou Mines. They have maintained their commitment to experimentation and collaboration, against all odds, for over twenty years. Admirers of their work value the group's genius for challenging established boundaries "between the 'cool' and the 'hot,' the visual and the verbal, the human and the technological, the popular and the elite, the individual and the collective," according to their promotional literature.

Theatre for the New City, 155 First Avenue, was born over twenty years ago in the West Village at Westbeth. The founders of Theatre for the New City performed for eight years at Westbeth and in the Judson Memorial Church auditorium. George Bartenieff and Crystal Field established the theatre in 1970 to embody the vision of a center for new and innovative theatre arts that would be truly accessible to the community, to discover relevant new writing, to bridge the gap between playwright, theatre artist, and the audience, and, finally, to bring the community into the theatre experience. It has a reputation for working with a variety of off-beat performing companies—as well as established companies—like the Bread & Puppet Theatre, Split Britches, The Talking Band, The Barking Rooster Company, Thunderbird American Indian Dancers, Off The Beaten Path, Red Mole Company, and the Theatre of Mistakes.

Bartenieff and Field seem to have snagged every award and citation in the history of off-Broadway. In addition to more than twenty-five OBIE awards, they have been cited for outstanding political theatre, outstanding director, outstanding performance, and outstanding design. Their distinguished alumni of actors, actresses, directors, playwrights, costume designers, choreographers, and lighting experts seems to include nearly everybody: Harvey Fierstein, Barbara Garson, Lawrence Kornfeld, Leonard Melfi, H. M. Koutoukas, Michael Smith, Robert Patrick, Rochelle Owens, Arthur Sainer, Sam Shepard, Richard Foreman, Ron Link, Paul Foster, Ron Tavel, Maria Irene Fornes, Ethyl Eichelberger, Anne Bogart, and hundreds more.

Theatre for the New City has an ongoing Internship Program as well as a Playwrights' Commissioning Program and a Summer Street Theatre Program. Perhaps its greatest event is the Annual Village Halloween Festival Ball. The building is transformed by sculptors, painters, and scenic designers into a series of Halloween environments, and simultaneous performances of every kind are held throughout the building and on the street outside the theatre. An average of 450 artists showcase their talents in this one-night-only extravaganza.

One of the more unusual pubs to crop up in the East Village is Café Sin-é (Gaelic for "That's It") at 122 St. Marks Place. Although there is no organized music here, the unorganized sessions that seem to occur spontaneously have taken on a life of their own. With a choice of but two beers, a limited menu devoted primarily to Irish stew, and a Bohemian, slightly anarchic atmosphere, this is the perfect place to escape New York and imagine you're one of James Joyce's Dubliners.

Tompkins Square Park, early 1960s

St. Marks Place ends at **Tompkins Square Park**. It is named for Daniel Tompkins, hero of the War of 1812 and progressive governor of New York, who was an early Abolitionist. The park was donated to the City in 1833 by the Stuyesvant family and has had a stormy history. Over the years, draft riots, union parades, and mass protest rallies have been held there. During the Vietnam War it was the site of numerous antiwar rallies and the site of historic rock concerts by the Grateful Dead and Country Joe and the Fish. Yippies and Hippies converging on the park generated mixed community feelings and attempts were made by the police to defuse wide-scale protests to prevent the park from being closed down.

In the 1990s, when people with no place to go set up housekeeping in the park, the community was once again in turmoil. The City administration closed the park permanently using as an excuse that it was being renovated. In a heartless and blind decision, the City tore down the historic bandstand to prevent people from using it as a shelter. No one expected Tompkins Square Park to be the site for a Children's Arbor Day event, like it was in 1904, but closing it down has served no real purpose except to deny the neighborhood of a park. The homeless have been forced to relocate to nearby lots and vacant buildings. One small loss is that a monument in the park commemorating the sinking of the excursion steamer General Slocum on June 15, 1904 will never be seen again. Most of those in the disaster were Germans from the neighborhood. After the disaster, the Germans moved uptown.

An easily overlooked, small bronze plaque affixed to the 3rd Street facade of the **First Houses** (on the southeast side of East 3rd Street and Avenue A) is the only notable sign of the architectural, cultural, and historic importance of these plain-looking four-and five-story brick buildings. First Houses was the first public, low-income housing project in the U.S. and the first housing project undertaken by the New York City Housing Authority, which was established by Mayor Fiorello La Guardia in 1934. Designed as an experimental rehabilitation program to deal with the terrible slums of the Lower East Side, the project was planned for 122 families, with an average monthly rental of $6.05 per room. All apartments had steam heat and hot water. Renter eligibility was based in part on family income, which was supposed to be more than five times the rent. Dedication of the new housing project was a national event, with radio coverage that included a telegram from President Franklin D. Roosevelt.

Frederick L. Ackerman was the architect for the First Houses, whose design included a secluded rear courtyard that runs the length of the buildings, making a delightful oasis unusual in any city neighborhood, much less the crowded Lower East Side. Animal sculptures, set in the brick walls, make charming decorations in the yard, and a low brick wall separates the yard from the rear of the 2nd Street buildings. First Houses is a designated New York City landmark.

The Living Theatre occupies a storefront at 272 East 3rd Street near Avenue C. It was incorporated by Judith Malina and her husband, the late Julian Beck, in 1947. It is New York City's oldest avant-garde repertory acting company and has established an international reputation. In addition to its theatre school, workshops, play readings, concerts, and street theatre, the Living Theatre has consistently presented some of the most imaginative and exciting productions seen on or off-Broadway since the era of the Provincetown Players.

The company took four years to gather its actors and technicians, opening officially in 1951 with Gertrude Stein's *Doctor Faustus Lights the Lights* at The Cherry Lane Theatre. On March 2, 1952, the

161

Julian Beck, Jackson MacLow, and Judith Malina at a peace rally at the Fillmore East, October 24, 1968

company opened with a program of "Bohemian Theatre" that included Stein's *Ladies Voices,* T. S. Eliot's *Sweeney Agonistes,* and, perhaps its most exciting production of the early '50s, an obscure Pablo Picasso play, *Desire or Trapped by the Tail.* Under the superb direction of Judith Malina, the play (with music by Lucia Dlugoszewski) astonished the critics and played to packed houses for fourteen weeks. Among the actors who played the "Two Bow-Wows" and "The Curtains" were two relatively unknown poets at the time, Frank O'Hara and John Ashbery. In succession followed Paul Goodman's *Faustina,* Alfred Jarry's farce *Ubu Roi,* and Ashbery's *The Heroes.* In 1954, with no money, the theatre moved to a cheap loft on upper Broadway and put on W.H. Auden's *The Age of Anxiety* and Luigi Pirandello's *Tonight We Improvise.*

After a long search and with the help of John Cage and Merce Cunningham, The Living Theatre found and converted an abandoned department store into its new home at 530 Sixth Avenue. The theatre was a major center in the late 1950s for fundraising and poetry readings by Black Mountain and Harvard poets and luminaries of the Beat Generation. On January 13, 1959, the new space opened with William Carlos Williams's verse comedy, *Many Loves*. But the play that first gained the Living Theatre international attention was Jack Gelber's highly controversial *The Connection* that appeared that summer and Kenneth H. Brown's *The Brig*.

The Living Theatre's most painful period came in October 1963 when the Internal Revenue Service seized the Sixth Avenue theatre for delinquent taxes of $20,000. A sit-in to prevent the seizure resulted in brief prison terms for the Becks and some members of the company. With no theatre, the group performed all over Europe and returned to New York in the late '60s to present four of their most resounding productions: *Paradise Now, Mysteries & Smaller Pieces, Frankenstein,* and *Antigone*. Stefan Brecht, the playwright, describes these plays this way:

> *Antigone* presents their anarchist theory of the state, *Frankenstein* that of history, *Mysteries & Smaller Pieces* is a review of the good and bad potentials of present day life and *Paradise Now* their theory of revolution—though it also more than the others creates in the theatre something like anarchist society by enacting something like the anarchist revolution.

In an early manifesto of the Living Theatre, the Becks wrote that:

> the theatre is love, drama, ritual, poetry, prose, reality. It is a place of intense experience, a thing in itself; it is a place where the spectator must participate by feeling and comprehending. It must be more than an entertainment. It is as terrifying and as amusing, as painful and as pleasurable as life is. It is a place in which one's senses are keenest. Everything that occurs is deeply aimed. The theatre is not an imitation of life. It is life itself.

The **Nuyorican Poets Café**, 236 East 3rd Street (between Avenues B and C), is the latest venue in the evolution of forums for poets and performance artists. Founded by Bob Holman and Miguel Algarin, the café is housed in a drafty, ground-floor, bare-brick loft. It offers a platform for the latest, self-indulgent post-Beats to recite their hip-hop indictments and celebrations of life in the 1990s. Some are just voices, some perform with live music, some with tapes, but rarely are they boring. Among the new young writers to have emerged from this spoken-word boom are Ed Morales, Mike Tyler, Tom Burnett, Luis Elaine Griffith, Paul Beatty, Willie Perdomo, Nicole Breedlove, Gail Schilke, Reggie Gaines, Pedro Pietri, and Sandra Maria Esteves.

Featuring the Poetry Slam, a sort of poetry Olympics with judges and scoring, Nuyorican attracts a cutting-edge crowd, describing itself as "an incredibly active scene. People hang out, dance, drink, and yell; the works are very urban, very rhythmic, full of sex, drugs, violence, politics, anger, humor." People come to the dark, lively space of Nuyorican to enjoy the bar, move to the music, and learn from the voices of the poets who each take their turn during the Poetry Slams, trying to win the ten-dollar prize. But remember, says host Bob Holman, "The best poet always loses."

Second Avenue/East 10th Street

Second Avenue; Yiddish Stage Stars; Eastern European Restaurants; Indian Restaurants; St. Marks-in-the-Bouwerie; 10th Street; The Club; Stuyvesant Fish House; Ottendorfer Library; Fillmore East; La Mama E.T.C.; New York City Marble Cemetery; Anthology Film Archives; Dorothy Day

Second Avenue from East Houston Street to Fourteenth Street was known in the 1930s as the Broadway of the Yiddish Theatre. The theatres specialized in melodrama and musical comedy, leaning heavily on success stories in which the immigrant makes good. More than twenty-five of the famous stars are immortalized with granite markers imbedded into the sidewalk in front of Abe Lebewohl's Second Avenue Kosher Deli just like on Hollywood Boulevard. Paul Muni, Maurice Schwartz, Molly Picon, Leo Fuchs, Mischa and Lucy Gehrman, Sholom Secunda, Peretz Sandler, Menashe Skulnick, Itzik Feld, Lucy Lux, Pesach Burstyn, Max and Rose Bozyk, Bella Meisel, and Jacob Adler are among the famous stars who performed on Second Avenue. Two of Adler's children, Luther and Stella, got their start on Second Avenue; they became leading actors and teachers.

Second Avenue is still famous for its ethnic restaurants. Eating places offer exotic menus of *borscht* (beet soup), *pirojski* (pastry), and *shashlik* (chunks of roasted lamb). Polish restaurants serve stuffed pig and *bigos mysliwski* (cabbage and game). And there are many reasonably priced Hungarian-Jewish, Rumanian, and Ukrainian restaurants where a meal includes chicken soup with *mandlen* (a kind of crouton) and stuffed *kishkes* (intestines).

Among the restaurants that have served the neighborhood for decades are The Kiev (117 Second Avenue at East 7th Street), a wonderful coffee shop that offers plentiful portions at bargain-basement prices; Ukrainian East Village (140 Second Avenue at East 9th Street); Christine's (208 First Avenue at East 12th Street); Teresa's Polish (103 First Avenue at East 6th Street); and the Second Avenue Kosher Deli (156 Second Avenue at East 10th Street), in a class by itself, famous for pastrami, tongue on rye, brisket, corned-beef sandwiches, and delicious knishes. Also worth visiting is B&H Dairy Restaurant, 127 Second Avenue (at East 6th Street). Adhering to kosher laws, this coffee shop serves only dairy products, with no meat or meat-derivatives on the menu. It's a classic no-frills experience, from the decaying linoleum to the rickety stools. But the food—at unbeatable prices—is worth braving the atmosphere for.

But that's not all. On the south side of one block, East 6th Street between First and Second Avenues, there are nineteen Indian restaurants, the largest number in one place in the entire world (except, maybe, Bombay!) The attention, the ambience, the excellent menu choices abound in each restaurant and many have live music: Mitali, Sonali, Gandhi, Prince of India, Bombay, and Calcutta are just a few of the fine eateries here.

The Polish, Jewish, Eastern European, Puerto Rican, and African-Americans who live in the neighborhood have contributed to its exciting, diverse atmosphere. The melting pot seems to be a most amicable one, for while the new Bohemians, old Hippies, and lost Beatniks are enjoying the European flavor and modest rent of the East Village, the older residents seem to feel the rejuvenating effects of youth and creativity.

St. Marks-in-the-Bouwerie, a church with a turbulent past, stands in the triangle at 10th Street and Second Avenue. Built in 1660, it was originally the private chapel on Peter Stuyvesant's bouwerie, or farm. In 1795, the cornerstone of the present Florentine and Venetian structure was laid on the site of the original chapel. The tower was added to the church in 1807, the steeple in 1826, the stone portico in 1836, and the cast-iron portico in 1858.

Besides Peter Stuyvesant, the peglegged Dutch governor of New Amsterdam whose remains are imbedded into the church's five-foot thick east wall, and all of his direct descendants, many famous persons are buried in the church graveyard. Among them is (or was) Commodore Matthew Calbraith Perry, the naval officer who during the 1850s negotiated Japan's first trade and diplomatic agreement with the U.S. Although officials of the Japanese consulate for many years laid flowers on his grave, no one in St. Marks was aware that Perry was buried there. Someone finally asked the Japanese whose grave they were honoring. A quick and embarrassed check of the records indicated that the grave belonged to Perry, and the Commodore's tomb was properly inscribed. But, in 1955, the vault was opened and the remains were not there. Perry is believed to be buried in Newport, Rhode Island.

St. Marks graveyard figured in a sensational headline story involving the theft by kidnapers of the remains of A. T. Stewart. The millionaire, founder of the store that eventually became Wanamaker's, died in 1876. His vault was placed twelve feet underground and was sealed with three heavy slabs. Nevertheless, enterprising ghouls stole the embalmed remains and held them for a ransom of $25,000. Stewart's widow negotiated for the body for two years, gave up, and finally, in 1880, the body was mysteriously returned after the widow had paid over $20,000. The bones were reinterred in a Garden City vault equipped with a burglar alarm.

St. Marks has actively fostered civil rights, promoted voter registration, supported prison reform, and opened the nation's first lesbian health care clinic. In the arts, St. Marks has presented dance concerts, plays, performance art, and introduced the community to some of the most eventful marathon poetry readings in East Village history. The Poetry Project recently celebrated its twenty-fifth anniversary.

Tenth Street, from Second Avenue to Fourth Avenue, was a pioneer outpost of the Greenwich Village art community in the 1950s. The main attraction for the artists was inexpensive living lofts with huge work spaces, high ceilings, and big windows. The vitality generated by the young abstract artists revitalized the neighborhood. Their difficulty in finding established galleries brave enough to show their work led them to band together and run their own galleries.

Willem de Kooning outside of his East 10th Street studio, April 5, 1959; the Tanager Gallery is on the left

The Tananger Gallery at 90 East 10th Street opened in the fall of 1953. Its members included artists Alex Katz, William King, Sally Hazelet, Philip Pearlstein, Raymond Rocklin, Lois Dodd, Tom Wesselmann, and Angelo Ippolito. Other galleries opened up: The Camino; Area; March; Brata; Phoenix; James; Hansa; Aspects Gallery; Hilda Carmel; Stryke. The galleries, the neighborhood, the camaraderie all contributed to the vitality of the art produced there.

Tenth Street during the 1950s became identified with the new style of American Action painting. Here was the birth of Abstract Expressionism, the legendary New York School. Art critics Harold Rosenberg, Clement Greenberg, Dore Ashton, Tom Hess, and Irving Sandler helped the fledgling Abstract Expressionist movement grow by writing about and reviewing new art and artists, resulting in serious recognition of the new artists: Jackson Pollock, Willem de Kooning, Robert Motherwell, Helen Frankenthaler, Franz Kline, Jack Tworkov, Joan Mitchell, Grace Hartigan, Alice Neel, Mark Rothko, Lee

168

Krasner, Elaine de Kooning, Philip Guston, Barnett Newman, Adolph Gottlieb, Louise Nevelson, William Baziotes, and Theodore Stamos. With a few exceptions, most of the artists lived and exhibited their work at one time or another on 10th Street, but they all at one time went to **The Club.**

Before The Club, the principle rendezvous of the art community was The Waldorf Cafeteria on Sixth Avenue and 8th Street. In her book *Minor Characters,* Joyce Johnson remembers the place:

> It was a dreary-looking place. I remember it as being a uniform grey-brown. It had none of the chrome-and-brass-art-deco fittings of the Automat, or the bountifulness of the Jewish cafeterias like Hector's near Time Square . . . there was something poor about the Waldorf, despite its ironic name . . . it was always crowded with interesting grownups who had no visible means of support: artists, poets, communists and anarchists, guitar-pickers, jailbirds, scavengers.

Nighttime roundtable discussions drew together a post–World War II band of artists who were in the process of discarding traditional European and American concepts of academic art and seeking a more personal idiom.

In the late fall of 1949, soon after an article on Jackson Pollock appeared in *Life,* the Lower East Side artists' rising fears of the art world's domination by European art coalesced into a new organization. Meeting in Ibram Lassaw's studio at the corner of Sixth Avenue and 12th Street in 1949, a group of about twenty artists, including Willem de Kooning, Franz Kline, Milton Resnick, Philip Pavia, Conrad Marca-Relli, and Giorgio Cavallon, formed a club and contributed ten dollars apiece to rent a loft. Unable to agree on a name, they called themselves simply "The Club." Ostensibly, The Club was a social organization, born out of the artists' frustrated need for a place to meet and talk, to "escape the loneliness of their studios [and] meet their peers to exchange ideas of every sort," according to Irving Sandler, The Club's foremost historian.

To bring the art community together, The Club began Friday night panel discussions that involved the real struggle of the artist to achieve recognition and status for an art the public was not yet ready to accept, that is, Abstract Expressionism. After its first years at 39 East 8th Street, The Club, gaining a stronger membership, moved to

*The Club's New Year's party, 1958.
L to r: Mike MacDonald, Nancy
Martin, Harold Rosenberg, Peter
Martin, Franz Kline, Ted Joans, Jim
Cuciara*

20 East 14th Street, 74 Fourth Avenue at 10th Street, 144 Second Avenue, 20 St. Marks Place, and finally to 306 Mercer Street, just a few doors from its original home. In 1962 with the death of Franz Kline and the closing of the Cedar Street Tavern due to a fire, The Club dissolved and the scene ended.

Today there is nothing left of The Club, the 10th Street galleries, or the lofts where the famous artists lived. The rebellion was over, the battle was won. What remains is the legacy of the New York School that made possible, without ridicule or pain, all the art movements that followed.

Stuyvesant Fish House, 21 Stuyvesant Street (at Second Avenue) is a three-story brick Federal style building that was begun in 1803. It is a unique example of a fine urban dwelling of the period; the house is rich in historical associations and is in pristine condition. Built by Peter Stuyvesant, a great-grandson and namesake of the last Dutch Director-General of New Amsterdam, the house is on land that the Dutch West India Company granted to the first Peter Stuyvesant in 1651 and that passed to his descendants. The younger Peter Stuyvesant built the house for his daughter, Elizabeth, at the time of her marriage to Nicholas Fish.

Nicholas Fish served at Valley Forge during the Revolutionary War. He was a major at the age of eighteen and is believed to have been the youngest major in the history of the United States Army. Fish was a close friend of Alexander Hamilton and was one of the executors of his estate. Fish was also an intimate friend of General Lafayette who was entertained at 21 Stuyvesant Street on the evening of September 10, 1824 during his famous return to America fifty years after the Revolutionary War. Nicholas Fish's son, Hamilton Fish, was born at 21 Stuyvesant Street in 1808. Hamilton Fish served as Governor of New York, as a United States Senator, and for eight years as Secretary of State. Hamilton Fish, Jr., who was a New York Congressman, is the father of Hamilton Fish III, publisher of *The Nation.*

In the 1970s an ammunition depot was uncovered in the rear of the house in excellent condition. It is a domed, circular brick-walled vault twelve feet deep and twelve feet in diameter. In the early days of New York, prominent families such as the Stuyvesants and the Fishes were asked to store arms that could be used to quell riots and insurrections.

The **Ottendorfer Branch, New York Public Library,** 135 Second Avenue (at 8th Street) is the oldest branch library in Manhattan and one of the earliest buildings in the City constructed specifically as a public library. Designed in 1883–1884 by the German-born architect William Schickel, it is an example of late Victorian architecture exhibiting elements of both neo-Italian Renaissance and Queen Anne styles. Built in conjunction with the German Dispensary next door, the library was the gift of Anna and Oswald Ottendorfer, both of whom immigrated to New York in 1844. They purchased the German-language weekly newspaper, the *New Yorker Staats Zeitung,* that was founded in 1834. The Ottendorfers commissioned Schickel to design a dispensary building and a library, thereby serving both the physical and mental well-being of the German community.

William Schickel worked for architect Richard Morris Hunt. Schickel designed, in addition to the Ottendorfer Library, the notable brick commercial structure, number 93–99 Prince Street, in the Soho Cast Iron Historic District. Even before construction was completed, the Ottendorfers officially turned the library over to the New York Free Circulating Library. The concept of the free circulating library, to serve the poorer segments of the population, was just beginning to receive considerable attention in New York. The New York newspapers were filled with editorial criticism of the lack of library facilities, the failure to serve the poor, and the backwardness of New York in contrast with other cities in establishing a free public library.

The New York Free Circulating Library was first supported by private funds until public funding was added in 1887. Many prominent and wealthy New Yorkers helped to further the library including Andrew Carnegie, J. P. Morgan, Cornelius Vanderbilt, Jacob H. Schiff, Henry G. Marquand, and John Jacob Astor, the son of the founder of the Astor Library.

Janis Joplin and Big Brother and the Holding Company performing at the Fillmore East, August 2, 1968

The building shell at 105 Second Avenue was Bill Graham's **Fillmore East**, the quintessential New York rock 'n' roll palace of the 1960s. Graham, who escaped Nazi Germany and became America's leading promoter of rock musicians and who helped develop the mass rock-concert format that drew audiences totaling in the millions, was killed in a helicopter crash near San Francisco in 1991. The entrance to the old Fillmore East is now sealed with cinder blocks and the marquee has disappeared, but anyone who ever went there will not easily forget the extraordinary music, the excitement, the scene, and the community spirit. Going to the Fillmore East was a political statement, a cultural event, an expression of brotherhood and togetherness. The music brought everybody together.

This was a remarkable era when the stage of the Fillmore lit up with Janis Joplin and Big Brother and the Holding Company, Jimi Hendrix's Band of Gypsies, Jerry Garcia and the Grateful Dead, Grace Slick and the Jefferson Airplane, Joe Cocker and Mad Dogs and Englishmen, Leslie West and Mountain, Jim Morrison and The Doors, Pete Townsend and The Who, and John Fogerty and Creedence

Clearwater Revival. Innovative lighting effects, now a staple of rock concerts, were pioneered here by the resident Joshua Light Show. The Fillmore East was born and bred to present group music, and that's precisely what it did with style and class, until the lights were doused on Sunday, June 27, 1971.

The **La Mama E.T.C.** (Experimental Theater Club), 74 East 4th Street, a downtown theatre institution for thirty years, was founded by Ellen Stewart and has played a major role in the establishment of off-Broadway theatre in New York City. Its roots were in a tiny basement theatre at 321 East 9th Street, a place where new playwrights could show their work and where directors could experiment. Stewart's first dramatic offering was a version of Tennessee William's *One Arm* presented in July 1962. She attracted a loyal band of actors and playwrights who were like a family. She became the mother of the East Village theatre scene and a legend in her own time.

La Mama's fame was achieved by introducing plays by Lanford Wilson, Sam Shepard, Israel Horovitz, Ed Bullins, Charles Ludlum, Jean-Claude van Itatie, Tom Eyen, Rochelle Owens, and Tom O'Horgan who helped define the rowdy, influential alternative theatre of the 1960s. Harvey Fierstein's *Torch Song Trilogy* opened at La Mama, as did *Godspell,* and the Blue Man Group's *Tubes*.

At La Mama it was possible to see performers like Robert De Niro, Richard Dreyfuss, Danny DeVito, F. Murray Abraham, and Jill Clayburgh before they became famous. There is also an emphasis on international theatre, in a tradition highlighted by an Italian production of *The Golem* in Italian and Yiddish by a Korean theatre company.

Plagued by under-financing, La Mama is always on the threshold of closing down. Ellen Stewart doesn't complain, she just states the facts, "We have enormous bills, insurance costs run $48,000 a year and Con Edison about $60,000 for a ten-month year. The La Mama payroll is $5,500 a week, which covers twenty-one people who work in a gallery, rehearsal and office space and three theaters, all housed in four buildings spread out over the Lower East Side." In addition to artists' fees, there are telephone and supply bills to be met, she added, as well as payments on a small mortgage on one of the buildings, and the company's "real deficit," which Stewart puts at about $176,000. "We've gone deeper, and deeper, and deeper" in debt, she says. During the 1991–92 season, the theatre came within a hair's breadth of closing; only last-minute contributions saved this important cultural institution. In the life of any off-Broadway theatre, financial doom always lurks from production to production. La Mama's financial condition may be typical of many others, and everybody hopes that prosperity is just around the corner.

New York City Marble Cemetery, 52–74 East Second Street (at Second Avenue) founded in 1831, was the second nonsectarian burial ground in New York devoted to family vaults and was considered a fashionable burial ground. An earlier marble cemetery is around the corner on Second Avenue sandwiched between two buildings.

New York City Marble Cemetery was organized as a business venture by Evert Bancker, Samuel Whittemore, Henry Booraem, Garret Storm, and Thomas Addis Emmet, an Irish lawyer and patriot who is buried in St. Paul's churchyard. The cemetery is surrounded by a high cast-iron fence and by houses and tenements, but may be easily viewed through the handsome fence. The grounds contain 256 vaults and gravestones. Marble Cemetery has the remains of Stephen Allen, Mayor of New York City (1821–1824); Isaac Varian, another Mayor (1839–1841); Preserved Fish, a famous New York merchant; Marinus Willet, a Revolutionary War hero who commanded the forces of the Mohawk valley in 1780; and James Henry Roosevelt, who founded Roosevelt Hospital (see 478 Broadway). John Lloyd Stephens, who pioneered archaeological research in the Mayan country of Mexico in the 19th century, and John Ericsson, designer of the Ironclad Monitor, are also buried here. The best-known person buried in Marble Cemetery was President James Monroe, who had moved to New York in 1830 after his wife died. He came to live with his son-in-law Samuel Gouverneur, who owned a vault in the cemetery. When Monroe died on July 4, 1831, he was one of the first to be buried at Marble Cemetery. Although a monument was erected over the vault, Monroe's body was dug up and reburied in Hollywood Cemetery in Richmond, Virginia.

Anthology Film Archives, open to the public at 32 Second Avenue (at 2nd Street), evolved from visions that go back to the early '60s, when Jonas Mekas, the director of the Film-Makers' Cinematheque, a showcase for avant-garde films, dreamed of establishing a permanent home where the growing number of new independent/avant-garde films could be shown on a regular basis. This dream became a reality in 1969 when Jerome Hill, P. Adams Sitney, Peter

Kubelka, Stan Brakhage, and Mekas drew up plans to create a museum dedicated to the vision of the art of cinema as guided by the avant-garde sensibility.

Anthology Film Archives opened in 1970 at the Public Theatre, moved to 80 Wooster Street, and then acquired Manhattan's Second Avenue courthouse building. Here Anthology found an ideal home as a chamber museum, dedicated to the preservation, study, and exhibition of independent and avant-garde film. It is the first museum devoted to film as an art form, committed to the guiding principle that a great film must be seen many times, that the film print must be the best possible, and that the viewing conditions must be optimal.

Anthology maintains that the "art of film must be defined in terms of selected works which indicate its essence and its possibilities." At the courthouse there have been retrospectives of the films of Hollis Frampton, Robert Breer, Yvonne Rainer, Robert Frank, Maya Deren, Alain Robbe-Grillet, Emile de Antonio, Barbara Rubin, Michael Snow, and Rudy Burckhardt. Anthology provides temporary homes for the Millennium Film Workshop, the Collective for Living Cinema, festivals of Native American Cinema, the Lesbian and Gay Experimental Film Festival, and several other independent groups.

During the last few years, Anthology's Independent Film Preservation program has been responsible for saving thousands of films— all independent productions—abandoned by film laboratories. Huge collections of filmic documents of life in America during the '50s, '60s, and '70s, and many avant-garde film classics, have been saved by Anthology's film preservation program. Finally, Anthology's reference library contains the world's largest collection of paper materials documenting the history and practice of American and international avant-garde and independent film and video. The files contain original documents, manuscripts, letters, scripts, notebooks, clippings, photographs, and stills.

The Courthouse Gallery serves as an exhibition space for film and videomakers who are also working as painters, photographers, or sculptors such as Harry Smith, Peter Hutton, Paul Sharits, Marjorie Keller, Carolee Schneemann, Ricky Leacock, and many others.

Dorothy Day, a radical social reformer, lived at 36 East First Street. She came to New York in 1914, after two years at the University of Illinois. A deeply religious young woman, she got a job at the socialist publication *Call* by promising she would live on the Lower East Side on five dollars a week and write about the misery and sufferings caused by capitalism. By the time she was twenty, Dorothy Day discovered that "human suffering had become her ruling passion." She also assimilated the Village's Bohemian spirit, and was a familiar figure in the Hell Hole bar on Sixth Avenue, where, it is said, she could drink the bar's seedy patrons under the table. In 1927, she converted to Catholicism, and, to further her work for social justice, she produced the first issue of the progressive journal, *Catholic Worker,* which was distributed in Union Square on

Dorothy Day in her office at the Catholic Worker, *November 18, 1969*

May Day, 1933. Her goal was to promote the social teachings of the Church and to offer a permanent model of Catholic identity based upon a voluntary embracing of poverty and a deep personal piety. Among the movement's achievements was the founding of "houses of hospitality" for farmers and other workers hurt by the Depression. Day supported unionization for farm workers in the 1960s, and, as a pacifist, she was involved in protests against the Vietnam war. She died in 1980. The labor movement that she founded continues to work out of her old home.

Listings

Antique Dealers; Art Galleries; Bars and Pubs; Bookstores; Cafés and Coffeehouses; Movie Houses; Museums; Newspapers; Night Life; Poetry Places; Records/Tapes/CDs; Restaurants; Specialty Foods; Sports; Theatres/Performance Spaces

Here's a complete checklist of all of the stores, restaurants, museums, and clubs mentioned in the book, plus many others; all information is current as of publication date. Because New York is an ever-changing city, you would be well-advised to check for current addresses and phone numbers before embarking on a trip. Be aware that the galleries selected all have rotating shows and are not shops that peddle "art" or do framings. Also, the newspapers listed service the Village, but their headquarters may be located elsewhere; their phone numbers, but not their addresses, have been included in the listings.

For those unfamiliar with New York's street numbering, the City is divided into East and West quadrants by Fifth Avenue. As you progress away from Fifth Avenue in either direction, street address numbers increase. Thus 24 W. 12th Street would be directly west of Fifth Avenue. Of course, in the West Village where streets meander in often baffling ways, this system is not very useful. For this reason, we've given cross-streets to help you locate a specific place. For consistency's sake, all listings are alphabetical by last name; David Allan Enterprises is listed under "A" not "D," for example. However, the Carlin-Bindig Gallery would be alphabetized under "C" (because these are two surnames).

Antique Dealers

David Allan Enterprises	812 Broadway (E. 12th St.)	598-9030
Antique City	51 E. Houston St. (Mott St.)	219-2069
Atelier of Prague	465 Broome St. (West Broadway)	274-9455
Back Pages Antiques	125 Greene St. (Spring St.)	460-5998
Beneduce	281 Lafayette St. (Prince St.)	274-0411
Bertha Black	80 Thompson St. (Spring St.)	966-7116
Jacques Carcanagues, Inc.	19 Greene St. (Grand St.)	941-4781
Victor Carl Antiques	55 E. 13th St. (Broadway)	673-8740
Cobweb	116 W. Houston St. (Varick St.)	505-1558
Philip Colleck of London	830 Broadway (E. 12th St.)	505-2500
Dampierre & Co.	79 Greene St. (Spring St.)	966-5474
Depression Modern	150 Sullivan St. (Prince St.)	982-5699
Distant Origin	153 Mercer St. (Prince St.)	941-0024
Dullsville	143 E. 13th St. (Broadway)	505-2505
Eileen Lane Antiques	150 Thompson St. (Bleecker St.)	475-2988
Evergreen Antiques	120 Spring St. (Greene St.)	966-6458
Full House	133 Wooster St. (Prince St.)	529-2298
Robert Gingold Antiques	95 E. 10th St. (University Pl.)	475-4008
Greene Street Antiques	65 Greene St. (Prince St.)	274-1076
Hamilton-Hyre, Ltd.	413 Bleecker St. (Bank St.)	989-4509
Hyde Park Antiques	836 Broadway (E. 12th St.)	477-0033
Irreplaceable Artifacts	14 Second Ave. (E. Houston St.)	777-2900
Kaleidoscope Antiques	636 Hudson St. (Horatio St.)	989-1036
Howard Kaplan Antiques	827 Broadway (E. 12th St.)	674-1000
René Kearne	322 Bleecker St. (Christopher St.)	727-3455
Karl Kemp & Associates	29 E. 10th St. (University Pl.)	254-1877
Kentshire	37 E. 12th St. (University Pl.)	673-6644
Keith Lane	77 Greene St. (Prince St.)	925-7414
Le Fanion	299 W. 4th St. (Bank St.)	463-8760
Le Passé au Présent	69 Spring St. (Lafayette St.)	274-0304
Leroma & Co.	135 Sullivan St. (Spring St.)	477-6304

Lost City Arts	275 Lafayette St. (Prince St.)	941-8025
H. M. Luther Inc.	61 E. 11th St. (Broadway)	505-1485
Lyme Regis Ltd.	68 Thompson St. (Spring St.)	334-2110
Maison Gerard	36 E. 10th St. (University Pl.)	674-7611
Martell Antiques	53 E. 10th St. (University Pl.)	777-4360
Lawrence Michael	816 Broadway (E. 11th St.)	529-8444
Modern Things	325 Lafayette St. (E. Houston St.)	219-1458
Mood Indigo	181 Prince St. (Thompson St.)	254-1176
Moss Alan Studios	88 Wooster St. (Spring St.)	219-1663
Susan Parrish	390 Bleecker St. (Perry St.)	645-5020
Peter Roberts Antiques	134 Spring St. (Wooster St.)	226-4777
Pierre Deux Antiques	369 Bleecker St. (Charles St.)	243-7740
Pine Country Antiques	71 Mercer St. (Broome St.)	274-9663
Renee Antiques	8 E. 12th St. (Fifth Ave.)	929-6870
Retro-Modern Studio	88 E. 10th St. (University Pl.)	674-0530
Second Childhood	283 Bleecker St. (Seventh Ave. S.)	989-6140
Second Coming	72 Greene St. (Spring St.)	431-4424
Second Hand Rose	270 Lafayette St. (Prince St.)	431-7673
Fred Silberman	83 Wooster St. (Spring St.)	925-9470
Niall Smith	344 Bleecker St. (W. 10th St.)	255-0660
Strand & Low	75 Thompson St. (Spring St.)	925-0932
T & K French Antiques	120 Wooster St. (Prince St.)	219-2472
Treasures & Trifles	409 Bleecker St. (Bank St.)	243-2723
The Tudor Rose	28 E. 10th St. (University Pl.)	677-5239
280 Modern	280 Lafayette St. (Prince St.)	941-5825
U.S.E.D.	17 Perry St. (Seventh Ave. S.)	627-0730
Urban Archeology	285 Lafayette St. (E. Houston St.)	431-6969
White & Howlett	71 Spring St. (Lafayette St.)	274-0034
Wooster Gallery	86 Wooster St. (Spring St.)	219-2190

Art Galleries

A/D	560 Broadway (Prince St.)	966-5154
Aesthetic Realism	141 Greene St. (W. Houston St.)	777-4490
Agora	560 Broadway (Prince St.)	226-4406
AICH	708 Broadway (Bleecker St.)	598-0100

A.I.R.	63 Crosby St. (Spring St.)	966-0799
Salvatore Ala	560 Broadway (Prince St.)	941-1990
Scott Alan	524 Broadway (Spring St.)	226-5145
Alex-Edmund	478 West Broadway (Prince St.)	260-5900
Brooke Alexander	59 Wooster St. (Broome St.)	925-4338
American Fine Arts	40 Wooster St. (Broome St.)	941-0401
Ameringer & Avard	155 Spring St. (West Broadway)	219-3108
Amos Eno	594 Broadway (Houston St.)	226-5342
Arena	128 Wooster St. (Prince St.)	226-1420
Art 54 Gallery	54 Greene St. (Broome St.)	226-1605
Art in General	79 Walker St. (Broadway)	219-0473
Artists Space	223 West Broadway (Franklin St.)	226-3970
Arts du Monde	154 Spring St. (Greene St.)	226-3702
Atlantic	164 Mercer St. (W. Houston St.)	219-3183
Pamela Auchincloss	558 Broadway (Prince St.)	966-7753
B4A Gallery	510 Broadway (Spring St.)	925-9735
Josh Baer	476 Broome St. (Greene St.)	431-4774
Vrej Baghoomian	555 Broadway (Prince St.)	941-1410
Jayne H. Baum	588 Broadway (Houston St.)	219-9854
David Beitzel	102 Prince St. (Greene St.)	219-2863
Bellas Artes	584 Broadway (Prince St.)	274-1116
Berland/Hall	579 Broadway (Prince St.)	274-9580
Berman/Daferner	568 Broadway (Prince St.)	226-8330
S. Bitter-Larkin	597 Broadway (Houston St.)	219-0150
Blue Mountain	121 Wooster St. (Prince St.)	226-9402
Blum Helman Warehouse	80 Greene St. (Spring St.)	226-8770
Mary Boone	417 West Broadway (Prince St.)	431-1818
Janet Borden	560 Broadway (Prince St.)	431-0166
Bowery	121 Wooster St. (Prince St.)	226-9543
Bridgewater/Lustberg	529 Broadway (Spring St.)	941-6355
Philippe Briet	558 Broadway (Prince St.)	334-0433
Broadway Windows (NYU)	Broadway at E. 10th St.	998-5751
Broome Street Gallery	498 Broome St. (West Broadway)	226-6085
Diane Brown	23 Watts St. (Thompson St.)	219-1060
Christine Burgin	130 Prince St. (Wooster St.)	219-8379
Frank Bustamante	560 Broadway (Prince St.)	226-2108

Leo Castelli	420 West Broadway (Prince St.)	431-5160
	65 Thompson St. (Spring St.)	219-2219
	578 Broadway (Prince St.)	431-6279
Castillo Gallery	500 Greenwich St. (Spring St.)	941-5800
Cavin-Morris	560 Broadway (Prince St.)	226-3768
CB's Gallery	313 Bowery (Bleecker St.)	677-0455
Center for Tapestry Arts	167 Spring St. (West Broadway)	431-7500
Ceres	91 Franklin St. (Broadway)	226-4725
Olaf Clasen	470 Broome St. (Greene St.)	334-0277
Cleaver Callahan	568 Broadway (Prince St.)	925-2350
Condeso/Lawler	76 Greene St. (Spring St.)	219-1283
Paula Cooper	149/155 Wooster St. (Prince St.)	674-0766
Coup de Grace	579 Broadway (Prince St.)	431-5799
Charles Cowles	420 West Broadway (Prince St.)	925-3500
Crown Point Press	568 Broadway (Prince St.)	226-5476
Dannenberg	484 Broome St. (Greene St.)	219-0140
James Danziger	415 West Broadway (Spring St.)	226-0056
Maxwell Davidson	415 West Broadway (Spring St.)	925-5300
Mary Delahoyd	426 Broome St. (Crosby St.)	219-2111
Dia Center—Broken Kilometer	393 West Broadway (Spring St.)	989-5912
Dia Center—Earth Room	141 Wooster St. (Prince St.)	989-5912
E. M. Donahoe	560 Broadway (Prince St.)	226-1111
Dooley Le Cappellaine	252 Lafayette St. (Prince St.)	431-3914
Fred Dorfman	123 Watts St. (Hudson St.)	966-4611
The Drawing Center	35 Wooster St. (Broome St.)	219-2166
Dyansen Eclipse	157 Spring St. (West Broadway)	925-6203
Vera Engelhorn	591 Broadway (Houston St.)	966-6882
Rosa Esman	575 Broadway (Prince St.)	219-3044
Exit Art	578 Broadway (Prince St.)	966-7745
Fawbush	76 Grand St. (Wooster St.)	274-0660
Feature	484 Broome St. (Greene St.)	941-7077
Ronald Feldman	31 Mercer St. (Grand St.)	226-3232
fiction/nonfiction	21 Mercer St. (Grand St.)	941-8611
55 Mercer	55 Mercer St. (Grand St.)	226-8513
First Street Gallery	560 Broadway (Prince St.)	226-9127

Flynn	113 Crosby St. (Prince St.)	966-0426
49th Parallel	420 West Broadway (Prince St.)	925-8349
14 Sculptors	164 Mercer St. (W. Houston St.)	966-5790
494 Gallery	494 Broadway (Broome St.)	925-9841
Fourth St. Photo	67 E. 4th St. (Second Ave.)	673-1021
Franklin Furnace Archive	112 Franklin St. (West Broadway)	925-4671
Gagosian	136 Wooster St. (Prince St.)	228-2828
Gallery Henoch	80 Wooster St. (Spring St.)	966-6360
Gallery Three Zero	30 Bond St. (Lafayette St.)	505-9668
Sandra Gering	476 Broome St. (Greene St.)	226-8195
Germans Van Eck	420 West Broadway (Prince St.)	219-0717
John Gibson	568 Broadway (Prince St.)	925-1192
Gimpel/Weitzenhoffer	415 West Broadway (Prince St.)	925-6090
Barbara Gladstone	99 Greene St. (Spring St.)	431-3334
Foster Goldstrom	560 Broadway (Prince St.)	941-9175
John Good	532 Broadway (Spring St.)	941-8066
Jay Gorney Modern Art	100 Greene St. (Spring St.)	966-4480
Howard Greenberg	120 Wooster St. (Prince St.)	334-0010
Grey Art Gallery (NYU)	33 Washington Pl. (Washington Sq. E.)	998-6780
Haenah-Kent	568 Broadway (Prince St.)	941-6180
Hanson	465 West Broadway (Prince St.)	353-2080
O. K. Harris	383 West Broadway (Spring St.)	431-3600
Emily Harvey	537 Broadway (Spring St.)	925-7651
Pat Hearn	39 Wooster St. (Broome St.)	941-7055
Helander	415 West Broadway (Spring St.)	966-9797
Heller	71 Greene St. (Broome St.)	966-5948
Nancy Hoffman	429 West Broadway (Prince St.)	966-6676
Humphrey	594 Broadway (Houston St.)	226-5360
Jamison/Thomas	588 Broadway (Houston St.)	925-1055
Nathalie Karg	100 Greene St. (Prince St.)	334-0436
Paul Kasmin	580 Broadway (Prince St.)	219-3219
Hal Katzen	475 Broome St. (Greene St.)	966-4469
June Kelly	591 Broadway (Houston St.)	226-1660
Kenkeleba	214 E. 2nd St. (Ave. B)	674-3939
Phyllis Kind	136 Greene St. (Prince St.)	925-1200

Nicole Klagsbrun	51 Greene St. (Broome St.)	925-5157
Klarfeld-Perry	472 Broome St. (Greene St.)	941-0303
Michael Klein	594 Broadway (Houston St.)	431-1980
John Post Lee	588 Broadway (Houston St.)	966-2676
Lennon Weinberg	580 Broadway (Prince St.)	941-0012
Chuck Levitan	42 Grand St. (Broadway)	966-2782
Stuart Levy	415 West Broadway (Spring St.)	941-0009
Lieberman & Saul	155 Spring St. (West Broadway)	431-0747
Amy Lipton	67 Prince St. (Crosby St.)	925-7140
Lorence Monk	568 & 578 Broadway (Prince St.)	431-3555
Louver	130 Prince St. (Wooster St.)	925-9205
Simon Lowinsky	575 Broadway (Prince St.)	226-5440
Virginia Lust	61 Sullivan St. (Broome St.)	941-9220
Curt Marcus	578 Broadway (Prince St.)	226-3200
Martin Lawrence	457 West Broadway (Prince St.)	995-8865
Martin Lawrence Modern	426 West Broadway (Prince St.)	941-5665
Louis K. Meisel	141 Prince St. (West Broadway)	677-1340
Metro Pictures	150 Greene St. (W. Houston St.)	925-8335
Midtown Y Photo Gallery	344 E. 14th St. (First Ave.)	674-7200
Miller	560 Broadway (Prince St.)	226-0702
Laurence Miller	138 Spring St. (Wooster St.)	226-1220
Molica Guidarte Gallery	379 West Broadway (Spring St.)	219-2244
Montserrat	584-588 Broadway (Houston St.)	941-8899
Robert Morrison	59 Thompson St. (Spring St.)	986-7180
Jain Marunouchi Gallery	560 Broadway (Prince St.)	274-8087
Newburg Gallery	580 Broadway (Prince St.)	219-1885
Noho Gallery	168 Mercer St. (W. Houston St.)	219-2210
David Nolan	560 Broadway (Prince St.)	925-6190
Nordanstad-Skarstedt	49 Greene St. (Broome St.)	274-1747
Annina Nosei	100 Prince St. (Greene St.)	431-9253
Opsis Foundation	561 Broadway (Prince St.)	966-8881
Pace Gallery	142 Greene St. (W. Houston St.)	431-9224
Franklin Parrasch	588 Broadway (Houston St.)	925-7090
Parsons School Exhibitions Center	66 Fifth Ave. (13th St.)	229-8987
Marilyn Pearl	420 West Broadway (Prince St.)	966-5506

Pen and Brush Club	16 E. 10th St. (Fifth Ave.)	475-3669
Katharina Rich Perlow	560 Broadway (Prince St.)	941-1220
Phoenix	568 Broadway (Prince St.)	226-8711
Pindar	127 Greene St. (Spring St.)	353-2040
Pleiades	164 Mercer St. (W. Houston St.)	274-8825
P.P.O.W.	532 Broadway (Spring St.)	941-8642
Prince Street	121 Wooster St. (Prince St.)	226-9402
Max Protech	560 Broadway (Prince St.)	966-5454
Puchong	36A Third Ave. (E. 10th St.)	982-1811
Robin Rice Gallery	325 W. 11th St. (Greenwich St.)	366-6660
Ricco/Maresca	105 Hudson St. (Franklin St.)	219-2756
Margarete Roeder	545 Broadway (Spring St.)	925-6098
Arthur Roger	136 Prince St. (Wooster St.)	966-4017
Andrea Rosen	130 Prince St. (Wooster St.)	941-0203
Stephen Rosenberg	115 Wooster St. (Prince St.)	431-4838
Rubenstein/Diacond	130 Prince St. (Wooster St.)	431-4221
Rubin Spangle	395 West Broadway (Broome St.)	226-2161
Sander Gallery	105 Hudson St. (Franklin St.)	219-2200
Sculptors Guild	110 Greene St. (Prince St.)	431-5669
Kathryn Sermas	19 Greene St. (Grand St.)	431-5743
Tony Shafrazi	130 Prince St. (Wooster St.)	274-9300
Jack Shainman	560 Broadway (Prince St.)	966-3866
Anita Shapolsky	99 Spring St. (Mercer St.)	334-9755
Snyder Fine Art	588 Broadway (Houston St.)	941-6860
Soho Photo Gallery	15 White St. (Sixth Ave.)	226-8571
Soho 20	469 Broome St. (Greene St.)	226-4167
Solo Gallery	578 Broadway (Prince St.)	925-3599
Sonnabend	420 West Broadway (Prince St.)	966-6160
Souyun Yi	249 Centre St. (Broome St.)	334-5189
Sperone Westwater	121 Greene St. (Prince St.)	460-5497
	142 Greene St. (W. Houston St.)	431-3685
Staempfli	415 West Broadway (Spring St.)	941-7100
Philippe Staib Gallery	8 Greene St. (Grand St.)	941-5977
Staley Wise	560 Broadway (Prince St.)	966-6223
Stark	594 Broadway (Houston St.)	925-4484
Bernice Steinbaum	132 Greene St. (Prince St.)	431-4224

SteinGladstone	99 Wooster St. (Spring St.)	925-7474
Step Gallery	66 Crosby St. (Spring St.)	226-6516
Stricoff Fine Art	118 Greene St. (Prince St.)	219-3977
Stux	155 Spring St. (West Broadway)	219-0010
Sunnen	49 Prince St. (Third Ave.)	966-3188
Synchronicity Space	55 Mercer St. (Grand St.)	925-8645
Edward Thorp	103 Prince St. (Greene St.)	431-6880
Thread Waxing Space	476 Broadway (Broome St.)	966-9520
303 Gallery	89 Greene St. (Spring St.)	966-5606
Barbara Toll	146 Greene St. (W. Houston St.)	431-1788
Tribeca 148	148 Duane St. (West Broadway)	406-4073
Tribeca Gallery	51A Hudson St. (Duane St.)	233-5858
Twining	568 Broadway (Prince St.)	431-1830
Visual Arts	137 Wooster St. (Prince St.)	598-0221
Vorpal	411 West Broadway (Prince St.)	334-3939
Ward-Nasse	178 Prince St. (Thompson St.)	925-6951
John Weber	142 Greene St. (W. Houston St.)	966-6115
Wheeler-Seidel	129 Prince St. (Wooster St.)	533-0319
White Columns	154 Christopher St. (Greenwich St.)	924-4212
Willow Gallery	470 Broome St. (Greene St.)	941-5743
Elga Wimmer	560 Broadway (Prince St.)	274-0274
Witkin	415 West Broadway (Spring St.)	925-5510
James Yu	393 West Broadway (Broome St.)	431-7867
Z Squared Fine Art Gallery	382 West Broadway (Broome St.)	334-1932
Andre Zarre	154 Wooster St. (Houston St.)	353-3456
Zona	97 Greene St. (Spring St.)	925-6750

Bars and Pubs

Anglers & Writers	420 Hudson St. (St. Luke's Pl.)	675-0810
Arthur's Tavern	57 Grove St. (Seventh Ave. S.)	675-6879
Automatic Slims	733 Washington St. (Bank St.)	645-8660
Back Fence	155 Bleecker St. (Thompson St.)	475-9221
Blanche's Bar	135 Avenue A (St. Marks Pl.)	673-3824
Bleecker Street Tavern	56 Bleecker St. (Lafayette St.)	334-0244
Boxer's	186 W. 4th St. (Barrow St.)	633-2275

Bradley's	70 University Pl. (E. 11th St.)	473-9700
Capitol Bar & Grill	14 Ave. A (E. 2nd St.)	254-1394
Cedar Street Tavern	82 University Pl. (W. 11th St.)	929-9089
Lee Chumley's	86 Bedford St. (Barrow St.)	675-4449
Corner Bistro	331 W. 4th St. (Eighth Ave.)	242-9502
Cowgirl Hall of Fame	519 Hudson St. (W. 10th St.)	633-1133
Dennis' Inn	137 Franklin St. (West Broadway)	925-7822
Down the Hatch	179 W. 4th St. (Sixth Ave.)	627-9747
Downtown Beirut	158 First Ave. (St. Marks Pl.)	260-4248
Duplex Cabaret	61 Christopher St. (Sheridan Sq.)	255-5438
Eagle Tavern	355 W. 14th St. (Hudson St.)	924-0275
Ear Inn	326 Spring St. (Greenwich St.)	226-9060
Fanelli's Bar	94 Prince St. (Mercer St.)	226-9412
Googie's	237 Sullivan St. (W. 3rd St.)	673-0050
Grassroots Tavern	20 St. Marks Pl. (Third Ave.)	475-9443
Joe's Bar & Grill	142 W. 10th St. (Seventh Ave. S.)	727-1785
Julius's Tavern	159 W. 10th St. (Waverly Pl.)	929-9672
Kastro Lounge	237 E. 5th St. (Second Ave.)	475-4949
Kenn's Broome Street Bar	363 West Broadway (Broome St.)	925-2086
Kettle of Fish	130 W. 3rd St. (Sixth Ave.)	533-4790
Lion's Head Ltd.	59 Christopher St. (Sheridan Sq.)	929-0670
Marie's Crisis	59 Grove St. (Seventh Ave. S.)	243-9323
McGovern's Bar	305 Spring St. (Sixth Ave.)	627-5037
McSorley's Old Ale House	15 E. 7th St. (Third Ave.)	473-9148
Milady's	162 Prince St. (Thompson St.)	226-9340
Minetta Tavern	113 MacDougal St. (W. 3rd St.)	475-3850
Peculiar Pub	145 Bleecker St. (La Guardia Pl.)	353-1327
Puffy's Tavern	81 Hudson St. (Greenwich St.)	766-9159
Riverrun Café	176 Franklin St. (Hudson St.)	966-3894
Riviera Café	225 W. 4th St. (Seventh Ave. S.)	242-8732
7A Café	109 Ave. A (E. 7th St.)	673-6583
Slaughtered Lamb Pub	182 W. 4th St. (Morton St.)	727-3350
Speakeasy	107 MacDougal St. (Bleecker St.)	598-9670
The Stoned Crow	85 Washington Pl. (Sixth Ave.)	677-4022
Telephone Bar & Grill	149 Second Ave. (E. 9th St.)	529-5000
Vazac's Horseshoe Bar	108 Ave. B (E. 7th St.)	677-6742

Village Corner	142 Bleecker St. (La Guardia Pl.)	473-9762
Village Gate	160 Bleecker St. (Thompson St.)	475-5120
Village Vanguard	178 Seventh Ave. S. (Perry St.)	255-4037
Walker's	16 N. Moore St. (Varick St.)	941-0142
Wetlands	161 Hudson St. (Laight St.)	966-4225
White Horse Tavern	567 Hudson St. (W. 11th St.)	989-3956
Z-Bar	206 Ave. A (E. 12th St.)	982-9173

Bookstores

A Different Light	548 Hudson St. (Charles St.)	989-4850
Bar and Books	636 Hudson St. (Jane St.)	229-2642
Biography Book Shop	400 Bleecker St. (W. 11th St.)	807-8655
Books of Wonder	464 Hudson St. (Barron St.)	645-8006
Cooper Square Books	21 Astor Pl. (Fourth Ave.)	533-2595
B. Dalton Bookseller	396 Sixth Ave. (W. 8th St.)	674-8780
East West Books	78 Fifth Ave. (14th St.)	243-5994
	67 Cooper Sq. (Fourth Ave.)	475-4459
Esoterica	61 Fourth Ave. (E. 9th St.)	529-9808
Forbidden Planet	821 Broadway (E. 13th St.)	473-1576
Foul Play Books of Mystery & Suspense	10 Eighth Ave. (W. 12th St.)	675-5115
Gay Treasures Inc.	546 Hudson St. (Christopher St.)	255-5756
Granary Books	568 Broadway (Prince St.)	226-5462
John Williams Book Store	171 Sullivan St. (Bleecker St.)	674-9036
Judith's Room	681 Washington St. (Charles St.)	727-7330
Mercer St. Books	206 Mercer St. (Bleecker St.)	505-8615
Mosaic Books	167 Ave. B (E. 10th St.)	475-8623
New York Open Center Bookstore	83 Spring St. (Broadway)	219-2527
NYU Bookstore	18 Washington Pl. (Greene St.)	998-4667
Oscar Wilde Memorial Bookshop	15 Christopher St. (Gay St.)	255-8097
Pageant Books	109 E. 9th St. (Fourth Ave.)	674-5296
Perimeter	146 Sullivan St. (Bleecker St.)	529-2275
A Photographers Place	133 Mercer St. (Spring St.)	431-9358

Printed Matter	77 Wooster St. (Spring St.)	925-0325
Revolution Books	13 E. 16th St.	691-3345
Jaap Rietman Inc.	134 Spring St. (West Broadway)	966-7044
Rizzoli Bookstore	454 West Broadway (Prince St.)	674-1616
St. Marks Bookshop	12 St. Marks Pl. (Third Ave.)	260-7853
Science Fiction Shop	163 Bleecker St. (Sullivan St.)	473-3010
Shakespeare & Co.	716 Broadway (Washington Pl.)	529-1330
Spring Street Books	169 Spring St. (West Broadway)	219-3033
Strand Book Store	828 Broadway (E. 12th St.)	473-1452
Sufi Books	227 West Broadway (White St.)	334-5212
Three Lives & Co.	154 W. 10th St. (Waverly Pl.)	741-2069
Tower Books	383 Lafayette St. (E. 4th St.)	228-5100
Untitled	159 Prince St. (West Broadway)	982-2088
Untitled II	680 Broadway (Bleecker St.)	982-1145
Ursus Art Books	375 West Broadway (Spring St.)	226-7858
Vanni Italian Books	30 W. 12th St. (Sixth Ave.)	675-6336
Village Comics	163 Bleecker St. (Sullivan St.)	777-2770
Fred Wilson Chess Books	80 E. 11th St. (Broadway)	533-6381

Cafés and Coffeehouses

Atelier	436 Hudson St. (Morton St.)	989-1363
Augie's Espresso Bar	107 Thompson St. (Prince St.)	966-5758
Bruno's	506 La Guardia Pl. (Bleecker St.)	982-2854
Café	210 Spring St. (Sixth Ave.)	274-0505
Café Borgia	185 Bleecker St. (MacDougal St.)	473-2290
Café Feenjon	40 W. 8th St. (MacDougal St.)	989-8686
Café Figaro	186 Bleecker St. (MacDougal St.)	677-1100
Café Lucca	222 Bleecker St. (Carmine St.)	675-7331
Café Mille Fleurs	246 W. 4th St. (Charles St.)	785-7946
Café Picasso	59 Bleecker St. (Charles St.)	929-6232
Café Tartine	253 W. 11th St. (W. 4th St.)	229-2611
Café Yaffa	97 St. Marks Pl. (Second Ave.)	674-9302
Caffè Cefalu	259 W. 4th St. (Charles St.)	989-7131
Caffè Dante	79 MacDougal St. (Bleecker St.)	982-5275
Caffè Dell'Artisti	46 Greenwich Ave. (W. 10th St.)	645-4431
Caffè Donatello	207 Waverly Pl. (Seventh Ave. S.)	242-1449

Caffè Giardino	25 Cleveland Pl. (Spring St.)	431-3806
Caffè Rafaella	134 Seventh Ave. S. (Charles St.)	929-7247
Caffè Reggio	119 MacDougal St. (W. 3rd St.)	475-9557
Caffè Vivaldi	32 Jones St. (Bleecker St.)	929-9384
Caliente Cab Co.	61 Seventh Ave. S. (Bleecker St.)	243-8517
Cornelia St. Café	29 Cornelia St. (Bleecker St.)	989-9319
The Cupping Room	359 West Broadway (Broome St.)	925-2898
Dean & Deluca University Pl.	75 University Pl. (W. 11th St.)	473-1908
Dean & Deluca Café	121 Prince St. (Mercer St.)	254-8776
Duane Park Café	157 Duane St. (Greenwich St.)	732-5555
Franklin Café	222 West Broadway (Franklin St.)	226-0172
Jon Vie Pastries & Café	492 Sixth Ave. (W. 12th St.)	242-4440
La Lanterna Caffè	129 MacDougal St. (W. 4th St.)	777-9074
Le Petit Café	156 Spring St. (West Broadway)	219-9723
Little Mushroom Café	183 W. 10th St. (W. 4th St.)	242-1058
Olive Tree Café	117 MacDougal St. (W. 3rd St.)	254-3630
Patisserie Claude	187 W. 4th St. (Sheridan Sq.)	255-5911
Patisserie Lanciani	271 W. 4th St. (Perry St.)	929-0739
Peacock Café	24 Greenwich Ave. (Charles St.)	242-9395
Penguin Café	581 Hudson St. (Abingdon Sq.)	627-7277
Veniero Pasticceria	342 E. 11th St. (First Ave.)	674-7264
Washington Market Café	162 Duane St. (Hudson St.)	571-4500

Movie Houses

Angelika Film Center	18 W. Houston St. (Mercer St.)	995-2000
Anthology Film Archives	32 Second Ave. (E. 2nd St.)	505-5181
Art Greenwich Cineplex Odeon	97 Greenwich Ave. (W. 12th St.)	929-3350
Charas	605 E. 9th St. (Ave. C)	533-6835
Cinema Village 12th St.	22 E. 12 St. (Fifth Ave.)	924-3363
Cinema Village Third Ave.	100 Third Ave. (E. 12th St.)	505-7320
8th Street Playhouse	52 W. 8th St. (Sixth Ave.)	674-6515
Film Forum 2	209 W. Houston St. (Sixth Ave.)	727-8110
Le Cinematographe	15 Vandam St. (Varick St.)	675-4592

Loews East Village	66 Third Ave. (E. 11th St.)	982-0400
Millennium	66 E. 4th St. (Bowery)	673-0090
Public Theatre	425 Lafayette St. (Astor Pl.)	598-7171
Quad Cinema	34 W. 13th St. (Fifth Ave.)	255-8800
Theatre 80	80 St. Marks Pl. (First Ave.)	254-7400
399 Westside Hwy	399 Westside Hwy. (W. 10th St.)	691-3720
U.A. Movieland	36 E. 8th St. (University Pl.)	477-6600
Village East	189 Second Ave. (E. 12th St.)	529-6799
Waverly Twin Cineplex Odeon	323 Sixth Ave. (W. 3rd St.)	929-8037

Museums

Alternative Museum	594 Broadway (Houston St.)	966-4444
Forbes Magazine Galleries	62 Fifth Ave. (W. 12th St.)	206-5548
Guggenheim in SoHo	575 Broadway (Prince St.)	334-5330
Lower East Side Tenement Museum	97 Orchard St. (Grand St.)	431-0233
Museum of Colored Glass & Light	72 Wooster St. (Spring St.)	226-7258
New Museum of Contemporary Art	583 Broadway (Houston St.)	219-1355
New York City Fire Museum	278 Spring St. (Varick St.)	691-1303
Old Merchant's House	29 E. 4th St. (Third Ave.)	777-1089
Ukrainian Museum	203 Second Ave. (E. 7th St.)	228-0110

Newspapers

Artspeak	924-6531
Bomb	431-3943
Cover	673-1152
Downtown	529-2255
Downtown Resident	679-1850
Manhattan Spirit	268-8600
New York Native	627-2120

New York Press	941-1130	
Night Howl	529-2255	
Paper	226-4405	
Village Voice	475-3300	
Villager	420-1660	

Night Life

Amazon Club	Pier 25 (N. Moore St.)	227-2900
Amazonas	492 Broome St. (Wooster St.)	966-3371
Arthur's Tavern	57 Grove St. (Seventh Ave. S.)	675-6879
Back Fence	155 Bleecker St. (Thompson St.)	475-9221
The Bank	225 E. Houston St. (Ave. A)	505-5033
Bitter End	149 Bleecker St. (La Guardia Pl.)	673-7030
Blue Note	131 W. 3rd St. (Sixth Ave.)	475-8592
Bond Street Café	6 Bond St. (Broadway)	979-6565
Boston Comedy Club	82 W. 3rd St. (Sullivan St.)	477-1000
Bottom Line	15 W. 4th St. (Mercer St.)	228-6300
Bradley's	70 University Pl. (E. 11th St.)	473-9700
Café Sin-é	122 St. Marks Pl. (First Ave.)	982-0370
Café Tabac	232 E. 9th St. (First Ave.)	674-7072
Café Wha?	117 MacDougal St. (Minetta La.)	254-3630
Cat Club	76 E. 13th St. (Fourth Ave.)	505-0090
CBGB&OMFUG	315 Bowery (Bleecker St.)	983-4052
Chase Bar & Grill	98 Third Ave. (E. 12th St.)	475-1407
Chicago B.L.U.E.S.	73 Eighth Ave. (W. 13th St.)	255-7373
Comedy Cellar	117 MacDougal St. (W. 3rd St.)	254-3630
Continental Divide	25 Third Ave. (E. 14th St.)	529-6924
Cottonwood Café	415 Bleecker St. (Bank St.)	924-6271
Downtown Beirut	158 First Ave. (St. Marks Pl.)	260-4248
Duplex Cabaret	61 Christopher St. (Sheridan Sq.)	255-5438
Eagle Tavern	355 W. 14th St. (Hudson St.)	924-0275
Eighty-Eight's	228 W. 10th St. (Bleecker St.)	924-0088
Five Oaks	49 Grove St. (Seventh Ave. S.)	243-8885
Gonzalez y Gonzalez	625 Broadway (Houston St.)	473-8787
Greene St.	101 Greene St. (Prince St.)	925 2415

191

Jack Dempsey's	61 Second Ave. (E. 3rd St.)	388-0662
Kenny's Castaways	157 Bleecker St. (Sullivan St.)	473-9870
Kelly's Village West	46 Bedford St. (Carmine St.)	929-9322
Knickerbocker	33 University Pl. (E. 9th St.)	228-8490
Knitting Factory	47 E. Houston St. (Mulberry St.)	219-3055
Ludlow Street Café	85 Ludlow St. (Prince St.)	353-0536
Marie's Crisis	59 Grove St. (Seventh Ave. S.)	243-9323
McGovern's Bar	305 Spring St. (Hudson St.)	627-5037
McSorley's Old Ale House	15 E. 7th St. (Third Ave.)	473-9148
Mission	531 E. 5th St. (Ave. B)	254-2610
Mondo Cane Blues Club	205 Thompson St. (Bleecker St.)	254-5166
Mondo Perso Blues Club	167 Bleecker St. (Sullivan St.)	477-3770
Mostly Magic	55 Carmine St. (Bleecker St.)	924-1472
Nell's	246 W. 14th St. (Hudson St.)	675-1567
New Frontier	61 W. 13th St. (Fifth Ave.)	366-5246
New Music Café	380 Canal St. (West Broadway)	941-1019
Nightingale Club	213 Second Ave. (E. 13th St.)	473-9398
Palladium	126 E. 14th St. (Third Ave.)	473-7171
Puffy's Tavern	81 Hudson St. (Greenwich St.)	766-9159
Pyramid Club	101 Ave. A (E. 7th St.)	420-1590
Rock N Roll Café	149 Bleecker St. (La Guardia Pl.)	677-7630
Roulette	228 West Broadway (White St.)	219-8242
S.O.B.s	204 Varick St. (Houston St.)	243-4940
Speakeasy	107 MacDougal St. (Bleecker St.)	598-9670
Spiral	244 E. Houston St. (Ave. A)	353-1740
Sticky Mike's Frog Bar	380 Lafayette St. (Great Jones St.)	533-3000
Sugar Reef	93 Second Ave. (E. 6th St.)	477-8427
Sun Mountain	82 W. 3rd St. (Thompson St.)	477-0622
Sweet Basil	88 Seventh Ave. S. (Bleecker St.)	242-1785
Terra Blues	149 Bleecker St. (Thompson St.)	777-7776
Time Café	380 Lafayette St. (Bond St.)	533-7000
Tribeca Lab	79 Leonard St. (West Broadway)	966-9371
Trocadero Café	368 Bleecker St. (Charles St.)	242-0636
Under Acme	9 Great Jones St. (Lafayette St.)	420-1934
Village Gate	160 Bleecker St. (Thompson St.)	475-5120
Village Vanguard	178 Seventh Ave. S. (Perry St.)	255-4037

Visiones	125 MacDougal St. (Bleecker St.)	673-5576
Wetlands	161 Hudson St. (Laight St.)	966-4225
Zinno	126 W. 13th St. (Seventh Ave.)	924-5182

Poetry Places

A Different Light	548 Hudson St. (Charles St.)	989-4850
American Indian Community House	708 Broadway (Bleecker St.)	598-0100
Cornelia St. Café	29 Cornelia St. (Bleecker St.)	989-9319
Dead Comics Society	230 E. 9th St. (Third Ave.)	629-2016
Dixon Place	258 Bowery (E. Houston St.)	219-3088
Ear Inn	326 Spring St. (Greenwich St.)	226-9060
Franklin Furnace Archive	112 Franklin St. (West Broadway)	925-4671
Hudson Park Library	10 Seventh Ave. S. (Carmine St.)	243-6876
Jefferson Market Library	425 Sixth Ave. (W. 10th St.)	243-4334
Judith's Room	681 Washington St. (Charles St.)	727-7330
Le Poeme	14 Prince St. (Elizabeth St.)	941-1106
Mosaic Books	167 Ave. B (E. 10th St.)	475-8623
New York Open Center	83 Spring St. (Broadway)	219-2527
Nuyorican Poets Café	236 E. 3rd St. (Ave. B)	505-8183
Pen and Brush Club	16 E. 10th St. (Fifth Ave.)	475-3669
Poetry Project at St. Marks	131 E. 10th St. (Second Ave.)	674-0910
Poets House	72 Spring St. (Broadway)	431-7920
Public Theatre	425 Lafayette St. (Astor Pl.)	598-7188
Time Café	380 Lafayette St. (Great Jones St.)	533-7000

Records/Tapes/CDs

Bleecker Bob's	18 W. 3rd St. (MacDougal St.)	475-9677
DanceTracks	91 E. 3rd St. (First Ave.)	228-3104
Disc-O-Rama	186 W. 4th St. (Morton St.)	206-8417
Downtown Music Gallery	211 E. 5th St. (Third Ave.)	473-0043
Finyl Vinyl	89 Second Ave. (E. 4th St.)	533-8007
Footlight Records	113 E. 12th St. (Third Ave.)	533-1572

Golden Disc	239 Bleecker St. (Cornelia St.)	255-7899
House of Oldies	35 Carmine St. (Bedford St.)	243-0500
It's Only Rock N Roll	49 W. 8th St. (MacDougal St.)	777-7090
Kim's Underground	144 Bleecker St. (La Guardia Pl.)	260-1010
Mercer St. Books and Records	206 Mercer St. (Bleecker St.)	505-8615
Music Inn	169 W. 4th St. (Sixth Ave.)	243-5715
Nostalgia Jazz	217 Thompson St. (Bleecker St.)	420-1940
Psychedelic Solution	33 W. 8th St. (MacDougal St.)	529-2462
Revolver Records	45 W. 8th St. (MacDougal St.)	982-6760
Rock's In Your Head	157 Prince St. (West Broadway)	475-6729
St. Marks Sounds	20 St. Marks Pl. (Third Ave.)	677-3444
Second Coming Records	235 Sullivan St. (W. 3rd St.)	228-1313
Smash Compact Discs	17 St. Marks Pl. (Third Ave.)	473-2200
Strider Records	22 Jones St. (Bleecker St.)	675-3040
Tower Records	692 Broadway (E. 4th St.)	505-1500
Venus Records	13 St. Marks Pl. (Third Ave.)	598-4459

Restaurants

Key to restaurant abbreviations

AM	American	IND	Indian
BBQ	Barbecue	IT	Italian
BEL	Belgian	JAP	Japanese
CAJ	Cajun	ME	Middle Eastern
CRB	Caribbean	MEX	Mexican
CUB	Cuban	NAT	Natural
DELI	Kosher-style deli	SF	Seafood
ECL	Eclectic	SP	Spanish
EEUR	Eastern European	SW	Southwest
ENG	English	TH	Thai
FR	French	VIET	Vietnamese

Acme Bar & Grill	CAJ	9 Great Jones St. (Lafayette St.)	420-1934
Afghan Village	ECL	5 St. Marks Pl. (Third Ave.)	979-6453
Aggie's	AM	146 W. Houston St. (MacDougal St.)	673-8994

194

Amazon Village	AM	Pier 25, West St. (Canal St.)	227-2900
Amici Miei	IT	475 West Broadway (Houston St.)	533-1933
Amsterdam's	AM	454 Broadway (Broome St.)	925-6166
Anar Bagh	IND	338 E. 6th St. (First Ave.)	529-1937
Angelica Kitchen	NAT	300 E. 12th St. (Second Ave.)	228-2909
Anton's	ECL	259 W. 4th St. (Perry St.)	675-5059
Arcobaleno	IT	21 E. 9th St. (Fifth Ave.)	473-2215
Arlecchino	IT	192 Bleecker St. (MacDougal St.)	475-2355
Arqua	IT	281 Church St. (White St.)	334-1888
Arturo's	IT	106 W. Houston St. (Thompson St.)	677-3820
Asti Restaurant	IT	13 E. 12th St. (Fifth Ave.)	741-9105
A Taste of India	IND	181 Bleecker St. (Sullivan St.)	982-0810
Auntie Pasta	IT	413 Greenwich St. (Hubert St.)	431-6945
	IT	611 Hudson St. (Abingdon Sq.)	645-8622
Au Troquet	FR	328 W. 12th St. (Greenwich St.)	924-3413
B&H Dairy	EEUR	127 Second Ave. (E. 6th St.)	505-8065
Ballato	IT	55 E. Houston St. (Mott St.)	274-8881
Barocco	IT	301 Church St. (Walker St.)	431-1445
Barolo	IT	398 West Broadway (Spring St.)	226-1102
Bayamo	CUB	704 Broadway (W. 4th St.)	475-5151
Beatrice Inn	IT	285 Worth St. (W. 4th St.)	929-6165
Bell Café	NAT	310 Spring St. (Hudson St.)	334-2355
Benny's Burritos	MEX	93 Ave. A (E. 6th St.)	254-2054
	MEX	113 Greenwich Ave. (Jane St.)	727-0584
Bernard & Steven's	FR	277 Church St. (White St.)	966-9881
Bianchi & Margherita	IT	186 W. 4th St. (Cornelia St.)	242-2756
The Black Sheep	AM	344 W. 11th St. (Washington St.)	242-1010
Blue Mill Tavern	AM	50 Commerce St. (Bedford St.)	243-7114
Boca Chica	MEX	13 First Ave. (E. 1st St.)	473-0108
Bonini	IT	62 W. 9th St. (Fifth Ave.)	777-0670
Boom	FR	152 Spring St. (West Broadway)	431-3663
Bouley	FR	165 Duane St. (Greenwich St.)	608-3852
Broadway Café	AM	651 Broadway (Bond St.)	529-4191
Brother's Bar-B-Q	BBQ	228 W. Houston St. (Varick St.)	727-2775

Bubby's	NAT	120 Hudson St. (N. Moore St.)	219-0666
Buon Appetito	IT	281 Bleecker St. (Seventh Ave. S.)	633-2941
Café	FR	210 Spring St. (Sixth Ave.)	274-0505
Café de Bruxelles	BEL	118 Greenwich Ave. (W. 13th St.)	206-1830
Café Espanol	SP	172 Bleecker St. (Sixth Ave.)	505-0657
	SP	63 Carmine St. (Bleecker St.)	675-3312
Café Loup	FR	18 E. 13th St. (Fifth Ave.)	255-4746
Café Melville	AM	110 Barrow St. (Washington St.)	924-0110
Café Tabac	AM	232 E. 9th St. (Second Ave.)	674-7072
Cajun Joe's	CAJ	52 Third Ave. (E. 10th St.)	505-1433
Can	VIET	482 West Broadway (Houston St.)	533-6333
Capsouto Frères	FR	451 Washington St. (Canal St.)	966-4900
Caribe	CRB	117 Perry St. (Greenwich St.)	255-9191
Casa Lafemme	FR	150 Wooster St. (W. Houston St.)	505-0005
Cent'Anni	IT	50 Carmine St. (Bleecker St.)	989-9494
Chanterelle	FR	2 Harrison St. (Hudson St.)	966-6960
Chez Brigitte	FR	77 Greenwich Ave. (Bank St.)	929-6736
Chez Jacqueline	FR	72 MacDougal St. (W. Houston St.)	505-0727
Chez Ma Tante	FR	189 W. 10th St. (W. 4th St.)	620-0223
Chez Michallet	FR	90 Bedford St. (Grove St.)	242-8309
Christine's	EEUR	208 First Ave. (E. 12th St.)	505-0376
CIII	ECL	103 Waverly Pl. (MacDougal St.)	254-1200
The Cloister Café	AM	238 E. 9th St. (Second Ave.)	777-9128
The Coach House	AM	110 Waverly Pl. (Sixth Ave.)	777-0303
Collage	AM	314 Bleecker St. (Grove St.)	645-1612
Col Legno	IT	231 E. 9th St. (Second Ave.)	777-4650
Cottonwood Café	SW	415 Bleecker St. (Bank St.)	924-6271
Cowgirl Hall of Fame	SW	519 Hudson St. (W. 10th St.)	633-1133
Cucina Della Fontana	IT	368 Bleecker St. (Charles St.)	242-0636
Cucina di Pesce	IT	87 E. 4th St. (Second Ave.)	260-6800
Cucina Stagionale	IT	275 Bleecker St. (Sixth Ave.)	924-2707
Cuisine de Saigon	VIET	154 W. 13th St. (Sixth Ave.)	255-6003
Da Silvano	IT	260 Sixth Ave. (Bleecker St.)	982-0090
Day-O	CRB	103 Greenwich Ave. (W. 12th St.)	924-3161

Duane Park Café	AM	157 Duane St. (West Broadway)	732-5555
Ecco	IT	124 Chambers St. (West Broadway)	227-7074
Ed Debevic's	AM	663 Broadway (Bond St.)	982-6000
Eddie's Restaurant	AM	14 Waverly Pl. (Mercer St.)	420-0919
El Charro Espanol	SP	4 Charles St. (Greenwich Ave.)	242-9547
El Coyote	MEX	774 Broadway (E. 10th St.)	677-4291
Elephant & Castle	AM	68 Greenwich Ave. (W. 11th St.)	243-1400
El Faro	SP	823 Greenwich St. (Horatio St.)	929-8210
El Rincon de Espana	SP	226 Thompson St. (Bleecker St.)	260-4950
El Teddy's	MEX	219 West Broadway (Franklin St.)	941-7070
Ennio and Michael	IT	539 La Guardia Pl. (Bleecker St.)	677-8577
Est Est Est	IT	64 Carmine St. (Bedford St.)	255-6294
Fedora Restaurant	IT	239 W. 4th St. (Charles St.)	242-9691
Felix	ECL	340 West Broadway (Grand St.)	431-0021
Flamingo East	ECL	219 Second Ave. (E. 13th St.)	533-2860
Florent	FR	69 Gansevoort St. (Washington St.)	989-5779
Frank's Restaurant	AM	431 W. 14th St. (Ninth Ave.)	243-1349
Frutti di Mare	IT	84 E. 4th St. (Second Ave.)	979-2034
Fuji	JAP	62 Greenwich St. (Sixth Ave.)	675-6195
Gandhi	IND	345 E. 6th St. (Second Ave.)	614-9718
Gaylord	IND	87 First Ave. (E. 5th St.)	529-7990
Gene's Restaurant	AM	73 W. 11th St. (Sixth Ave.)	675-2048
Genji	JAP	56 Third Ave. (E. 10th St.)	254-1959
Georgia Boy Premium Products	AM	165 W. 4th St. (Sixth Ave.)	255-5725
Gonzalez y Gonzalez	SW	625 Broadway (Houston St.)	473-8787
Gotham Bar & Grill	AM	12 E. 12th St. (University Pl.)	620-4020
Grand Ticino	IT	228 Thompson St. (Bleecker St.)	777-5922
Great Jones Street Café	CAJ	54 Great Jones St. (Bowery)	674-9304
Greene Street Restaurant	AM	101 Greene St. (Prince St.)	925-2415

Grove Street Café	AM	53 Grove St. (Bleecker St.)	924-9501
Gulf Coast	CAJ	489 West St. (W. 12th St.)	206-8790
Gus' Place	AM	149-151 Waverly Pl. (Sixth Ave.)	645-8511
Harbour Grill	SF	37 Barrow St. (Seventh Ave. S.)	691-0480
Harlequin	SP	569 Hudson St. (W. 11th St.)	255-4950
Hasaki	JAP	210 E. 9th St. (Second Ave.)	473-3327
Haveli	IND	100 Second Ave. (E. 5th St.)	982-0533
Honmura An	JAP	170 Mercer St. (Prince St.)	334-5253
Hudson Grill	AM	350 Hudson St. (King St.)	691-9060
Il Cantinori	IT	32 E. 10th St. (University Pl.)	673-6044
Il Mulino	IT	86 W. 3rd St. (Thompson St.)	673-3783
Il Piccolo	IT	39 Greenwich Ave. (W. 10th St.)	989-4100
Il Ponte Vecchio	IT	206 Thompson St. (Bleecker St.)	228-7701
Indochine	VIET	430 Lafayette St. (Astor Pl.)	505-5111
Iso Restaurant	JAP	175 Second Ave. (E. 11th St.)	777-0361
I Trè Merli	IT	463 West Broadway (W. Houston St.)	254-8699
Jane Street Seafood Café	SF	31 Eighth Ave. (Jane St.)	242-0003
Japanese on Hudson	JAP	551 Hudson St. (Perry St.)	691-5379
Japonica	JAP	100 University Pl. (W. 12th St.)	243-7752
Jekyll and Hyde	AM	91 Seventh Ave. S. (Barrow St.)	989-7701
Jerry's	AM	101 Prince St. (Greene St.)	966-9464
Joe's Bar & Grill	AM	142 W. 10th St. (Waverly Pl.)	727-1785
John Clancy	SF	181 W. 10th St. (Seventh Ave. S.)	242-7350
John's of 12th Street	IT	302 E. 12th St. (Second Ave.)	475-9531
John's Pizzeria	IT	278 Bleecker St. (Seventh Ave. S.)	243-1680
Jour et Nuit	FR	337 West Broadway (Grand St.)	925-5971
Kenn's Broome Street Bar	AM	363 West Broadway (Broome St.)	925-2086
Khyber Pass	ECL	34 St. Mark's Pl. (Second Ave.)	473-0989
Kiev	EEUR	117 Second Ave. (E. 7th St.)	674-4040
Kin Khao	TH	171 Spring St. (West Broadway)	966-3939
K-Paul's	CAJ	622 Broadway (Houston St.)	460-9633
La Boheme	IT	24 Minetta La. (Bleecker St.)	473-6447

La Focaccia	IT	51 Bank St. (W. 4th St.)	675-3754
La Gauloise	FR	502 Sixth Ave. (W. 12th St.)	691-1363
La Jumelle	FR	55 Grand St. (Wooster St.)	941-9651
La Metairie	FR	189 W. 10th St. (W. 4th St.)	989-0343
La Ripaille	FR	605 Hudson St. (W. 12th St.)	255-4406
La Spaghetteria	IT	178 Second Ave. (E. 10th St.)	995-0900
La Strada	IT	78-80 E. 4th St. (Second Ave.)	353-8026
L'Aubiniere	FR	218 Lafayette St. (Spring St.)	274-1522
Lavo	TH	90 Third Ave. (E. 12th St.)	477-6955
L'Ecole	FR	462 Broadway (Grand St.)	219-3300
Le Pescadou	FR	18 King St. (Sixth Ave.)	924-3434
Levee	BBQ	76 E. 1st St. (First Ave.)	505-9263
Lion's Head	AM	59 Christopher St. (Sheridan Sq.)	929-0670
Lora	ECL	104 W. 13th St. (Sixth Ave.)	675-5655
Lucky Strike	FR	59 Grand St. (Wooster St.)	941-0479
Lupe's East LA Kitchen	MEX	110 Sixth Ave. (Watts St.)	966-1326
Madeline's	AM	177 Prince St. (Thompson St.)	477-2788
Magic Carpet	MEX	54 Carmine St. (Bedford St.)	627-9019
Manhattan Bistro	ECL	129 Spring St. (Greene St.)	966-3459
Manhattan Chili Company	AM	302 Bleecker St. (Grove St.)	206-7163
Marinella	IT	49 Carmine St. (Bedford St.)	807-7472
Marion's Continental	ECL	354 Bowery (Great Jones St.)	475-7621
Mary Ann's	MEX	86 Second Ave. (E. 5th St.)	475-5939
Marylou's	SF	21 W. 9th St. (Fifth Ave.)	533-0012
Mary's Restaurant	IT	42 Bedford St. (Carmine St.)	243-9755
Memphis Trio Pizzeria	IT	140 Charles St. (Washington St.)	989-7707
Mezzogiorno	IT	195 Spring St. (Sullivan St.)	334-2112
Mi Cocina	MEX	57 Jane St. (Hudson St.)	627-8273
Minetta Tavern	IT	113 MacDougal St. (W. 3rd St.)	475-3850
Mingala Burmese	ECL	21 E. 7th St. (Second Ave.)	529-3656
Miracle Grill	AM	112 First Ave. (E. 6th St.)	254-2353
Mitali East	IND	334 E. 6th St. (Second Ave.)	533-2508
Mitali West	IND	296 Bleecker St. (Barrow St.)	989-1367

Monte's Trattoria	IT	97 MacDougal St. (Bleecker St.)	228-9194
Montrachet	FR	239 West Broadway (Walker St.)	219-2777
Moondance Diner	AM	80 Sixth Ave. (Broome St.)	226-1191
New Deal	AM	152 Spring St. (West Broadway)	431-3663
Nick and Eddie	FR	203 Spring St. (Sullivan St.)	219-9090
NoHo Star	AM	330 Lafayette St. (Bleecker St.)	925-0070
Nosmo King	ECL	54 Varick St. (Canal St.)	966-1239
Odéon	FR	145 West Broadway (Thomas St.)	233-0507
Odessa	EEUR	117 Ave. A (St. Marks Pl.)	473-8916
Omen	JAP	113 Thompson St. (Prince St.)	925-8923
Onda	TH	430 Broome St. (Crosby St.)	925-4743
One If By Land	ECL	17 Barrow St. (Seventh Ave. S.)	228-0822
One Hudson Café	ECL	1 Hudson St. (Chambers St.)	608-5835
Orfeo	AM	16 Second Ave. (E. 1st St.)	673-2135
Paris Commune	FR	411 Bleecker St. (W. 11th St.)	929-0509
Passage To India	IND	308 E. 6th St. (Second Ave.)	529-5770
Phebe's Place	AM	361 Bowery (Bleecker St.)	473-9008
Pierre's	ECL	170 Waverly Pl. (Christopher St.)	929-7194
The Pink Teacup	AM	42 Grove St. (Bleecker St.)	807-6755
Pizzapiazza	IT	785 Broadway (E. 10th St.)	505-0977
Ponte's	ECL	39 Desbrosses St. (West St.)	226-4621
Porto Bello	IT	208 Thompson St. (Bleecker St.)	473-7794
Prince of India	IND	342 E. 6th St. (Second Ave.)	228-0388
Provence	FR	38 MacDougal St. (Prince St.)	475-7500
Quatorze	FR	240 W. 14th St. (Seventh Ave.)	206-7006
Raoul's	FR	180 Prince St. (Sullivan St.)	966-3518
Raoul's Brasserie & Grill	FR	225 Varick St. (W. Houston St.)	929-1630
Rectangle's	ECL	159 Second Ave. (E. 10th St.)	677-8410
Rio Mar	SP	7 Ninth Ave. (Little W. 12th St.)	243-9015
Riviera Café	AM	225 W. 4th St. (Seventh Ave. S.)	929-3250
Rosalie's	FR	531 Hudson St. (W. 10th St.)	206-7093
Rose Café	AM	24 Fifth Ave. (9th St.)	260-4118
Rosemarie's	IT	145 Duane St. (West Broadway)	285-2610
Rosolio	IT	11 Barrow St. (Seventh Ave. S.)	645-9224
Royal Canadian Pancake	AM	145 Hudson St. (Beach St.)	219-3038

Sabor	CUB	20 Cornelia St. (Bleecker St.)	243-9579
Savoy	ECL	70 Prince St. (Crosby St.)	219-8570
Sazarac House	CAJ	533 Hudson St. (Charles St.)	989-0313
Second Avenue Deli	DELI	156 Second Ave. (E. 10th St.)	677-0606
Sevilla	SP	62 Charles St. (Seventh Ave. S.)	929-3189
Shakespeare's	AM	180 MacDougal St. (W. 3rd St.)	979-6200
Shiki's	JAP	69 Seventh Ave. S. (Bleecker St.)	206-7024
Siracusa	IT	65 Fourth Ave. (E. 9th St.)	254-1940
SoHo Kitchen and Bar	AM	103 Greene St. (Prince St.)	925-1866
Sonali	IND	326 E. 6th St. (Second Ave.)	505-7517
Souen	NAT	210 Sixth Ave. (Prince St.)	807-7421
Soup's On Café	ECL	210 W. 10th St. (W. 4th St.)	727-7499
Spring Street Natural	NAT	162 Spring St. (Lafayette St.)	966-0290
Sugar Reef	CRB	93 Second Ave. (E. 5th St.)	477-8427
Taj	IND	310 E. 6th St. (Second Ave.)	505-8056
Taj Mahal	IND	328 E. 6th St. (Second Ave.)	529-2217
Takahashi	JAP	85 Ave. A (E. 6th St.)	505-6524
Taste of Tokyo	JAP	54 W. 13th St. (Fifth Ave.)	691-8666
Tatiana	FR	26 Wooster St. (Grand St.)	226-6644
Tea & Sympathy	ENG	108 Greenwich Ave. (W. 12th St.)	807-8329
Telephone Bar & Grill	ENG	149 Second Ave. (E. 9th St.)	529-5000
Temple Bar	IT	332 Lafayette St. (Bleecker St.)	925-4242
Tennessee Mountain	BBQ	143 Spring St. (Wooster St.)	431-3993
Teresa's Coffee Shop	EEUR	103 First Ave. (E. 6th St.)	228-0604
Thai House Café	TH	151 Hudson St. (Leigh St.)	334-1085
Time Café	ECL	380 Lafayette St. (Great Jones St.)	533-7000
Tommy Tang's	TH	323 Greenwich St. (Duane St.)	334-9190
Tompkins Park Restaurant	AM	141 Ave. A (E. 9th St.)	260-4798
Toons	TH	417 Bleecker St. (Bank St.)	924-6420
Tortilla Flats	MEX	767 Washington St. (W. 12th St.)	243-1053

Trattoria Due Torri	IT	99 MacDougal St. (Bleecker St.)	477-6063
Trattoria Due Torri II	IT	136 W. Houston St. (MacDougal St.)	979-5950
Tribeca Grill	AM	375 Greenwich St. (Franklin St.)	941-3900
Triplets Roumanian Steakhouse	EEUR	11-17 Grand St. (Sixth Ave.)	925-9303
Tropical Treat II	CRB	230 Thompson St. (Bleecker St.)	505-5145
Tutta Pasta	IT	504 La Guardia Pl. (Houston St.)	420-0652
	IT	26 Carmine St. (Bleecker St.)	463-9653
Two Boots	CAJ/IT	37 Ave. A (E. 2nd St.)	505-2276
Two Eleven	AM	211 West Broadway (Franklin St.)	925-7202
Ukrainian East Village	EEUR	140 Second Ave. (E. 9th St.)	529-5024
Universal Grill	ECL	44 Bedford St. (Leroy St.)	989-5621
Upstairs at the Downstairs	IT	531 Hudson St. (Charles St.)	206-7093
Urbino	IT	78 Carmine St. (Seventh Ave. S.)	242-2676
Vanessa	ECL	289 Bleecker St. (Seventh Ave. S.)	243-4225
Veselka	EEUR	144 Second Ave. (E. 9th St.)	228-9682
Villa Florence	IT	9 Jones St. (W. 4th St.)	989-1220
Villa Mosconi	IT	69 MacDougal St. (Bleecker St.)	673-0390
Village Atelier	FR	436 Hudson St. (Morton St.)	989-1363
Village Crown	NAT	96 Third Ave. (E. 12th St.)	674-2061
Village East Natural	NAT	2 St. Marks Pl. (Third Ave.)	533-9898
Village Natural	NAT	46 Greenwich Ave. (Sixth Ave.)	727-0968
Violeta's	MEX	220 W. 13th St. (Seventh Ave.)	255-1710
VP2	NAT	144 W. 4th St. (Sixth Ave.)	260-7130
Vucciria	IT	422 West Broadway (Prince St.)	941-5811
Walker's	AM	16 N. Moore St. (Varick St.)	941-0142
West Broadway Restaurant	FR	349 West Broadway (Grand St.)	226-5885
White Horse Tavern	AM	567 Hudson St. (W. 11th St.)	989-3956
Whole Wheat 'n Wild Berrys	NAT	57 W. 10th St. (Fifth Ave.)	677-3410

Ye Waverly Inn	AM	16 Bank St. (Greenwich Ave.)	929-4377
Zinno	IT	126 W. 13th St. (Sixth Ave.)	924-5182
Zoe	ECL	90 Prince St. (Mercer St.)	966-6722
Zutto	JAP	77 Hudson St. (Jay St.)	233-3287

Specialty Foods

Balducci's Market	424 Sixth Ave. (W. 9th St.)	673-2600
Bazzini Nuts	339 Greenwich St. (Jay St.)	334-1280
Ben's Cheese Shop	181 E. Houston St. (Orchard St.)	254-8290
Commodities Natural Foods	117 Hudson St. (N. Moore St.)	334-8330
Danal Provisions	2 Bank St. (Greenwich Ave.)	691-8083
Dean & Deluca Fine Foods	560 Broadway (Prince St.)	431-1691
Faicco Pork Store	260 Bleecker St. (Leroy St.)	243-1974
Henri's Gourmet Deli	357 Bleecker St. (Charles St.)	645-6698
Hot Stuff	227 Sullivan St. (W. 3rd St.)	254-6120
Indiana Market	80 Second Ave. (E. 4th St.)	505-7290
Integral Yoga Natural Foods	229 W. 13th St. (Seventh Ave.)	243-2642
Jefferson Market	455 Sixth Ave. (W. 10th St.)	675-2277
Joe's Dairy	156 Sullivan St. (W. Houston St.)	677-8780
Kurowycky Meat Products	124 First Ave. (E. 7th St.)	477-0344
Lilac Chocolates	120 Christopher St. (Bedford St.)	242-7374
McNulty's Tea & Coffee	109 Christopher St. (Bleecker St.)	242-5351
Milan Laboratories	57 Spring St. (Lafayette St.)	226-4780
Moishe's Kosher Bakery	181 E. Houston St. (Orchard St.)	475-9624
Murray's Cheese Shop	257 Bleecker St. (Cornelia St.)	243-3289
Myers of Keswick	634 Hudson St. (Horatio St.)	691-4194
Natures Village	58 W. 8th St. (University Pl.)	982-6635
Ottomanelli's Meat Market	285 Bleecker St. (Jones St.)	675-4217
Pete's Spice	174 First Ave. (E. 10th St.)	254-8773
Porto Rico Importing Co.	201 Bleecker St. (Sixth Ave.)	477-5421
Priscilla's Gourmet Shop	35A Jane St. (Eighth Ave.)	255-0952
Raffetto's Pasta	144 W. Houston St. (Sullivan St.)	777-1261

The Ravioli Store	75 Sullivan St. (Spring St.)	925-1737
Russ & Daughters	179 E. Houston St. (Orchard St.)	475-4880
Schapira Coffee Co.	117 W. 10th St. (Greenwich St.)	675-3733
Yonah Schimmel	137 E. Houston St. (First Ave.)	477-2858
Spring Street Market	111 Spring St. (Mercer St.)	226-4780
Sunrise Natural Foods	142 W. Houston St. (Sullivan St.)	254-4373
Veniero's Pasticceria	342 E. 11th St. (First Ave.)	674-7264
Vesuvio Bakery	160 Prince St. (West Broadway)	925-8248
Washington Market	162 Duane St. (Hudson St.)	571-4500
Whole Foods In SoHo	117 Prince St. (Greene St.)	673-5388
Zito Bread	259 Bleecker St. (Jones St.)	929-6139

Sports

Bowlmor Lanes	110 University Pl. (E. 12th St.)	255-8188
Corner Billiards	85 Fourth Ave. (E. 11th St.)	995-1314
Julian's Billiards	138 E. 14th St. (Irving Pl.)	475-9338
Le Q Billiards	36 E. 12th St. (Broadway)	995-8512
Marshall Chess Club	23 W. 10th St. (Fifth Ave.)	477-3716
Village Chess Shop	230 Thompson St. (W. 3rd St.)	475-9580
Village Tennis Courts	110 University Pl. (E. 12th St.)	989-2300

Theatre/Performance Space

Abe Burrows Theater	721 Broadway (Waverly Pl.)	998-1860
Actors Playhouse	100 Seventh Ave. S. (W. 4th St.)	691-6226
American Mime Theater	61 Fourth Ave. (E. 9th St.)	777-1710
Astor Place Theatre	434 Lafayette St. (Astor Pl.)	254-4370
Bouwerie Lane Theatre	330 Bowery (Bond St.)	677-0060
Castillo Cultural Center	500 Greenwich St. (Canal St.)	941-5800
Cherry Lane Theatre	38 Commerce St. (Bedford St.)	989-2020
Circle-in-the-Square	159 Bleecker St (Thompson St.)	254-6330
Circle Rep Theatre	99 Seventh Ave. S. (W. 4th St.)	924-7100
Courtyard Playhouse	39 Grove St. (Bleecker St.)	869-3530
CSC Reperory	136 E. 13th St. (Second Ave.)	677-4210

Cucaracha Theatre	500 Greenwich St. (Canal St.)	966-8596
Dance Space	622-626 Broadway (Bleecker St.)	777-8067
Dixon Place	258 Bowery (E. Houston St.)	219-3088
Downtown Art Company	64 E. 4th St. (Broadway)	737-1227
Elysium Theater Company	204 E. 6th St. (First Ave.)	713-5478
Jewish Repertory Theatre	344 E. 14th St. (First Ave.)	505-2667
Kampo Cultural Center	31 Bond St. (Third Ave.)	228-3063
La Mama Annex Theatre	66 E. 4th St. (Second Ave.)	475-7710
La Mama E.T.C.	74A E. 4th St. (Second Ave.)	475-7710
Living Theater	272 E. 3rd St. (Ave. C)	979-0604
Lucille Lortel Theatre	121 Christopher St. (Bedford St.)	924-8782
Charles Ludlum Theatre	1 Sheridan Sq. (W. 4th St.)	691-2271
Minetta Lane Theatre	18 Minetta La. (Sixth Ave.)	420-8000
NADA	167 Ludlow St. (E. Houston St.)	420-1466
New York Theatre Workshop	79 E. 4th St. (Second Ave.)	302-6989
Ohio Theatre	66 Wooster St. (Prince St.)	966-4844
One Dream Theatre	232 West Broadway (N. Moore St.)	219-1160
Ontological Hysteric Theater	105 Hudson St. (N. Moore St.)	941-8911
The Performance Garage	33 Wooster St. (Broome St.)	966-3651
Performance Space 122	150 First Ave. (E. 9th St.)	477-5288
Perry St. Theatre	31 Perry St. (W. 4th St.)	691-2509
The Playground	230 E. 9th St. (Second Ave.)	459-4281
Prometheus Theatre	239 E. 5th St. (Second Ave.)	477-8689
Provincetown Playhouse	133 MacDougal St. (W. 3rd St.)	477-5048
Joseph Papp Public Theatre	425 Lafayette St. (Astor Pl.)	598-7150
Roulette	228 West Broadway (White St.)	219-8242
Soho Repertory Theatre	46 Walker St. (Broadway)	869-3530
St. Marks Theatre Project	131 E. 10th St. (Second Ave.)	533-4650
Gertrude Stein Rep	44 Walker St. (Broadway)	662-4495
Susan Stein Shiva Theatre	425 Lafayette St. (Astor Pl.)	598-7150
Sullivan Street Playhouse	181 Sullivan St. (Bleecker St.)	674-3838
Synchronicity Space	55 Mercer St. (Grand St.)	925-3960

Theatre for the New City	155 First Ave. (E. 10th St.)	254-1109
13th St. Theatre	50 W. 13th St. (Fifth Ave.)	675-6677
Tribeca Lab	79 Leonard St. (Broadway)	966-9371
Variety Arts Theatre	110 Third Ave. (E. 13th St.)	239-6200
Village Gate	160 Bleecker St. (La Guardia Pl.)	475-5120
Westbeth Theatre	151 Bank St. (West St.)	674-1369
Wings Theatre Company	154 Christopher St. (Greenwich St.)	627-2961

Index

211

Wilson, Edmund, 70, 89, 94
Wilson, Lanford, 58, 173
Wilson, Martha, 107
Wolf, Daniel, 82, 140, 154
Women's liberation movement, 10
Wooster Group, The, 102
Wright, Richard, 21

Y–Z

Yiddish Theatre, stars of, 165
Young, Izzy, 65

Young, Stark, 70
Yuppification, 10–11

Zaloom, Paul, 107, 158
Zeckendorf Tower, 131
Ziegel, Vic, 77
Zimmerman, Robert. *See* Dylan, Bob
Zion, Sid, 77
Zito, A., & Son, 58
Zogbaum, Wilfred, 154
Zorn, John, 145